Embroidery Machine Profits

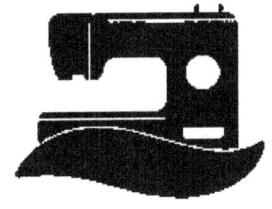

By TREV HUNT

DEDICATION

This book is dedicated to you, the reader. I hope you find it insightful & interesting enough to take the plunge into the world of Embroidery.

CONTENTS

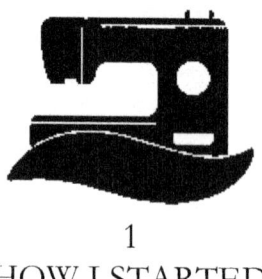

1
HOW I STARTED

The information contained within this book has changed my life for the better, and I feel compelled to share it with you. There's more than enough room for a similar business to operate in your neck of the woods, and I hope you'll join me in a truly enjoyable business you can start from home and build into a profitable enterprise. The information is set out in a sequential manner, with each section leading logically to the next. Please try to refrain from skipping ahead, as you'll undoubtedly miss many important snippets that I've included along the way. This book is not an A to Z of embroidery (I've already done one of those!), there's no ridiculous list of irrelevant things, no overly technical language to learn, and you don't need any previous experience or qualifications. Having said that, you will need to learn new skills, you will need to practice and fine tune those skills, and it helps to learn a few basic terms. But don't worry too much for now, as I am currently building up the Embrocraft YouTube channel with tutorials and other useful things to help you along the way. We'll come back to that in a later chapter.

How I got into this business

You have just stumbled into the strangest little

business I've ever encountered, and I've tried quite a few different ventures over the last 30 years. I was introduced to selling embroidered patches by accident. My brother had a much older friend & mentor, who'd been selling Motorsport Regalia at UK events since before I was born. Even though he's now crossed over to the big racetrack in the sky, we'll call him John to protect his identity. John had been doing the rounds of UK events for many years, but had grown tired of it. He'd also developed many other business interests and no longer had the time or the inclination to travel to events anymore. Eventually my brother agreed to run it part-time for a few years in return for a share of the proceeds.

The setup consisted of a double-axle trailer kitted out as a mobile shop, fully stocked with T-shirts, Baseball caps, Pin Badges, Stickers & a large selection of motorsport themed embroidered patches. We had a bit of fun with it, and travelled around many of the best race circuits in the UK & Ireland, Brands Hatch, Silverstone, Goodwood etc.

Those types of events tend to last anywhere from a few days to a full week. At the end of each day, the public get thrown out and the traders & racing teams get locked in. That's when the partying starts in the hospitality tents. Our usual plan was to swagger into these drinking tents, which often housed a free bar, complete with dancefloor, DJ and a whole bunch of party animals. Nobody knew who we were and nobody ever asked, we just joined in and got very drunk for free. Waking up in the back of the Jeep with a hangover was par for the course at these places. I once met racing driver Damon Hill at an event in Ireland! I was standing next to a very expensive

Classic Bentley that he mistakenly thought was mine! - I told him that I *wished* it was mine, to which he laughed, then carried on his way.

That part time sales job eventually came to an end after just a few years, but it was fun while it lasted.

Many years and several failed ventures later, I had a Brainfart while reminiscing those good old days, and made the decision to open an online shop selling embroidered patches. I didn't have a lot of hope for it in the beginning, but as it would not cost much to set up, I thought it might be worth a try anyway. So after an extensive search of suppliers, I bought in a good range of popular designs and built the first online shop. Although the website still exists, I've since closed this shop as I now have other business interests that take up most of my time.

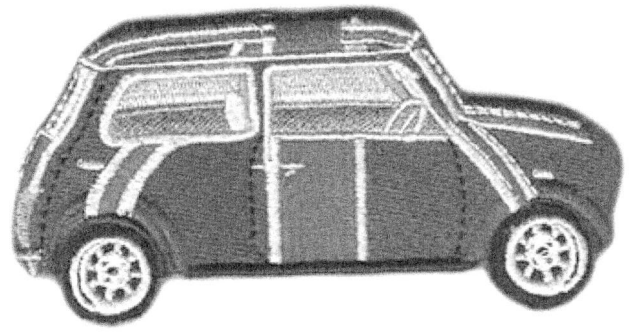

That's also the very reason I can now divulge the information contained in this book. It was hard won information that took several years and considerable expense to uncover. Many mistakes were made along the way, but that can often lead to significant progress.

You may be surprised to learn that after reading half a dozen books on building websites and search engine optimization by the so called 'experts', I realized that not much of their advice actually works in real life, things were just not panning out that way in the real world. The information would frequently appear to make sense, but the truth is that if everyone who applied those techniques built a successful website, we'd all be back to square one.

I eventually went against the web guru sourced advice in many different ways. The end result was that I created an online shop that bagged its first order from Google organic search traffic, just two weeks after it was built, with no prior advertising required. It started slow at first, with one sale every few days, then it grew steadily over the next few months into regular daily sales of 5 to 10 orders. There are many simple ways to achieve that growth and it's entirely possible build quite a substantial site and go much further. My main website started with just 75 product listings during those first few months, four years later it had grown to over 4000 product listings.

There's a whole lot more to this business than just retail sales, but as you will soon discover, retail sales can be a gateway into other things.

Those experts I referred to earlier will also tell you that opening an online shop is akin to opening a shop in your garden shed, ie, nobody will know it's there. That may have been true with older style HTML websites, but there are more dynamic ways to build a website in 2020, and faster ways to get a new website indexed, though you'd be wise to know that some very poor options also exist.

There are some pretty big sharks in the sea of online shop hosting, who on the surface appear to be fantastic, but are near useless in reality. It's only fair to inform you that the world of webhosting is chock full of liars and charlatans. My experience of them warrants an extra book in itself, so I'll curb this rant before I get carried away with the many stories of webhosting trickery and deception I've witnessed.

Those same Web Guru's I mentioned earlier will also tell you that it's nearly impossible to survive as a seller outside the sales platforms of eBay & Amazon, as those big sites have it all sewn up (please excuse the pun). Well the sum of my life experience has taught me that if you blindly put your faith & fate into the hands of other people, they will not just let you down, but will frequently stick the boot in as well. If you currently sell on those platforms, you'll do well to note that it's actually *their* business, not yours. I know of one eBay seller who had a turnover of £50k per month selling recycled goods, and eBay shut them down in one day over a trivial dispute. In the space of one night, that guy lost everything and his 10 staff lost their jobs. I've seen that happen a dozen times to people I know personally over the years. I'm a 7 times, eBay veteran, with over 20 years experience selling Computers, Electronics, CD's, DVD's PC Components & Embroidered Patches on eBay, and also a few years of selling products on Amazon. I'm not a one-hit-wonder, I've been selling online for the greater part of my adult life.

Here's a few interesting facts for you:

If you sell anything on eBay these days, you can expect a refund rate of between 4% to 10 %. My own theory is that the percentage depends entirely on how many refund monkeys it takes to change a lightbulb. But here's the kicker, Paypal only allow a refund rate of 3%. eBay has changed significantly in recent years and you have detailed seller ratings and listing allowances as well as feedback, so if you trade on eBay, you're almost guaranteed to get kicked off eventually, the odds are just not working in your favor. I recently read somewhere that eBay management don't like the idea of sellers getting *too* big on their site, and now you know how they prevent that from happening. The last time I checked, the vision they had for the future of eBay is 'One large online department store containing all the top brands'. It would appear that 99% of current eBay sellers won't be a part of that grandiose vision. It's certainly food for thought, but not the end of the world as there's more than one way to skin a Rabbit (we don't usually do cats in the UK).

If you're currently having a sneak preview of this book through the Amazon look inside feature, this is probably close to the point where you must decide to buy or fly. I assure you that it does get better from here onwards, and it's also why I'm holding back a little on the good stuff.

The thing to remember about the sales element of this information, is that it can easily be applied to selling other products, in other industries. The methods and mindset are probably the most important elements to remember, you can always choose to apply them to your own ideas in any way you wish.

Before we go any further, I will offer a quick insight into the origins of Embroidery.

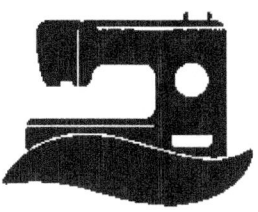

2

A BRIEF HISTORY OF EMBROIDERY

The word Embroidery stems from the French word for Embellishment, which is *Broderie*. But the art of Embroidery has been around almost as long as clothing itself.

Historical evidence shows that Ancient Egyptians, Babylonians, Phoenicians and Hebrews, all used embroidery for decorating their robes.

The Moors also frequently embellished much of their clothing with embroidery. Their unique style quickly spread to other countries like Spain and Sicily. Moorish embroidery went on to greatly influence the embroidery styles of many European countries.

The oldest embroidery works still in existence date back to the Middle Ages when embroidery was often used in ecclesiastical vestments as well as clothing. It also represented a sign of wealth, and rich traders and merchants were willing to pay a hefty sum for the luxury of embroidered clothing. A great example from this period is the Bayeux Tapestry, which is 20 inches tall and 231 feet long.

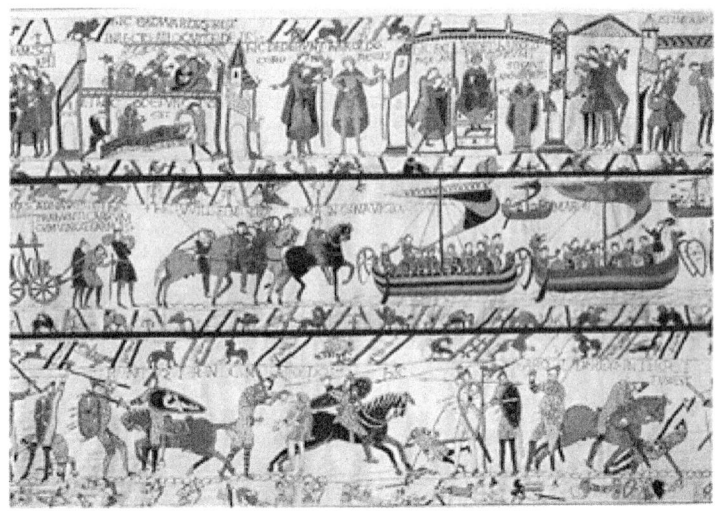

It tell the story (in pictures) of the events (from the Norman point of view) leading up to and including the Battle of Hastings, on October 14th, 1066.

Then we move on to the mighty armies of the world, who've used Embroidery to embellish their uniforms for thousands of years. From simple embroidered cloth badges worn to denote rank, status and achievements, to epaulettes and cap decoration.

The rather modern idea of Embroidery as a hobby, began in the Baronial homes of the wealthy elite in the 19th century, then eventually became a hobby for poorer folk over time.

The upper class women used the best fabrics, threads and garnishing's available, the poorer folk often used cheaper fabrics and whatever they could scavenge for the project, with cheap beads and sequins added for extra glamour.

Fast forward to 2020 and hand embroidery is still popular today, but it's a time consuming hobby that's unsuitable for any commercial enterprise.

I could very easily wade deeper into a more detailed history of embroidery, but I promised it would be brief and I'm fully aware that you didn't buy this book for a history lesson. You're reading this because you want to know how to make money with an embroidery machine, so this is the end of the chapter. To keep you from boredom, we must move swiftly on. How brief was that?

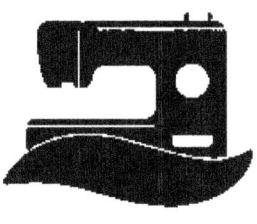

3

EMBROIDERED PATCHES

A little known fact is that embroidered patches creep into just about every aspect of our lives. It's also not necessarily a localized business, I've had customers from all over the world, from

Individuals to Multi-Nationals. The image shown above was from a project I made for an Antarctic expedition team. I've also completed many projects for television and film, and even the European Space Agency. There are also the many projects I can't mention, for various government departments who shall not be mentioned. This truly is a very interesting business indeed.

The information contained within this book can be applied to starting an embroidery businesses wherever you live in the world. Have a look at the quick list I've thrown together below, it's just a very small selection of sources within the United Kingdom, that I've had work from over just the last 10 years.

The British Army
The Royal Air Force
The Royal Navy
The NHS (UK National Health Service)
Town Councils
Hospitals
Schools
Colleges
Universities
Film Studios
Theatre Companies
The BBC

Dance Schools
Football Clubs
Sports Teams of every imaginable type.
Security Companies
Regional Police Forces
Individual Police Units
Individual officers
Biker Clubs
Airsoft Teams
PR Companies
Advertising Agencies
Design Studios
Graphic Designers
Publishers
New Clothing Companies (lots of them)
Local Tradesmen
Charities (every type imaginable)

I've stopped here because the list just goes on forever. If that list seems extensive to you, just add in the knowledge that it's entirely possible you'll get orders from similar entities in others Countries too. I've had a lot of work from random organizations within the European Union, to Oil Companies in the Middle East, to Scuba Diving Schools in Australia. It is ever changing and surprisingly interesting. If you could only see the caliber of the people in my email contact list, from high ranking officials to

CEO's of household name brands and the UK's leading Charities, it is ridiculous.

To my absolute amazement, I was once invited to partner up with Harrods of London, and Vogue Magazine to supply embroidered patches for a feature they were doing at London Fashion Week. I kid you not!. The worst part is that I had to turn them down because I'd overstretched myself with a long backlog of orders and simply didn't have enough time to make the products they needed. My daughters will still not forgive me for turning down both Vogue Magazine, a fashion industry leader *and* Harrods, the most expensive department store in London.

While that one didn't quite work out for me, another similar promotional opportunity did come good. I was approached by another fashion Magazine the following year to provide them with a selection of products from my then online retail shop. The agreement they offered was that I supply them with a temporary loan of some patch products, then in return they would credit my business as the supplier in the magazine feature. It made sense to me to forge a temporary alliance with the editor in return for a free advert, and as a sweetener I told them to keep the 70 or so items I'd sent, and the girls in their office were delighted they'd received some freebies. A few weeks later I got a complimentary copy of their magazine through the door (really not my thing, I don't read women's magazines) with a note asking me to have a look and express my opinion on the feature. I will tell you truthfully that I nearly dropped a brick when I saw that feature for the first time. A full double page spread, with world famous supermodels wearing patch laden designer clothes. These were all patch designs from my range, and only available from me! Ka-Ching!!! In one corner there was a small article expressing their thanks to me for supplying them, with a link to the shop, and my sales went through the roof for about 6 weeks before it tailed off again. I had no idea it would be that good! Nobody had ever mentioned supermodels to me, if they had I might have demanded to turn up at the photoshoot to inspect the goods or something?, (I could have been famous!).

A Word of Caution! It's worth noting that not all opportunities of this nature justify the time, effort and expense. A few similar promotions since that one, came to nothing. You have to judge each one individually and decide if it's in your best interests or theirs to participate.

If the sound of dealing with company directors

and high ranking officials scares the living shit out of you, then don't fret, there will always be plenty of normal customers to brighten up your day. Making projects for bigger fish is just one of many options. When you have a very small business and someone asks you to make a very large order, it's sometimes better to turn them down. I've noticed a trend over the years that when I do turn projects down, they tend to come back hungrier than ever! I do have a tendency to turn an unworkable project into an order I can live with, at a price they can afford and I can make good money on. Then everybody wins.

You need to be especially careful when it comes to dealing with government departments and large corporate entities. The inexperienced trader will accept anything they are offered by them and will be eternally grateful. I have always approached those same orders in a different way.

I don't give them credit accounts, I demand payment with order, then make them agree to my terms and my price, or they can Foxtrot Oscar. You then quickly discover how desperate they are to get their project made.

I once had to phone a Chief Constable (head of a UK police force) to tell him that his £2500

(USD$3000) badge order was ready, but he wasn't getting them unless they paid me pronto. Their bank transfer arrived the same day, as if by magic. I know it was a ballsy move to get my invoice paid, but sometimes people appreciate the honesty when you level with them. In my eyes they are all just people wearing costumes, and I supply the decorations.

Businesses fail every day. Any business that provides a service and then must wait 90 days to get paid from some government department or large multi-national corporation, is especially vulnerable. Sometimes the big fish try to wrangle out of it, they ask to renegotiate the price after the fact, or they just don't ever pay you. I fell for it in the early days, but quickly learned how to deal with them.

Here's an example of how I handled them:

Customer: We'll issue a purchase order and settle the bill at the end of the month (or quarter).

Me: 'I know you're used to dealing with things that way, but I trade on my own terms. You must agree to them and provide payment with the order if you wish to proceed. I'll put your purchase order number on the invoice, then you can get the payment sorted.'

 8 out of 10 just accept the terms and pay, the rest were probably going to shaft me on the invoice. That's how I sort the wheat from the chaff. My way or the highway.

That's a quick insight into what it can be like to run an online shop, selling your own unique range of stock embroidered patches. If it suits your lifestyle, you could easily open an online store and just simply buy in products to resell, no machinery required. If you buy your stock somewhere (online) in the Far East like Thailand or China, and sell in the UK or USA, retail sales can be quite profitable too, with up to 1000% markup on many items. I'll tell you exactly where to find those sources in a later chapter. If you're currently wondering how the hell you're going to build an online shop, I'll be giving you a little guiding help with that also, it's not quite as difficult as you might think.

The real shocker for me was when I stopped selling on eBay & Amazon and built my own online shop. Compared to those two huge sales platforms, new customers behaved very differently in my shop. If you're not familiar with selling on Amazon or eBay, there's something you really need to know in advance.

The customers you get on Amazon, are quite different than customers found on eBay. Amazon buyers are seemingly more reserved & mature, but as such, it's much harder to get sales. In complete contrast, eBay is frequented by far too many refund monkeys in my humble opinion. When I finally took the time to reconsider the following points:

1) How much the item cost to buy in.
2) How much both eBay & Paypal were taking in fees.
3) The cost of the free delivery which is now expected of sellers.
4) The real cost of returns and refunds.
5) The growing competition from Chinese sellers who are willing to take just a few pennies in profit to dominate a niche on these platforms.

Once I'd taken all of those points into account, there was no profit left for me.

Having started out selling products on those two big sites, it often annoyed me how I would get regular sales, but it was nearly always for one solitary item at a measly total of around GBP£3.

If you've ever sold lot's of low priced items via eBay & Paypal, you'll already know their fee structure does not favor low value items, it can be crippling for sellers of such products.

Once I'd escaped the clutches of the 'big two' and built my own online shop, the fun really started, as the sales arriving via my own customers were fantastic in comparison. I retained the services of Paypal for my own website, because with 300 million customers worldwide, even I can't ignore the fact that they do some things very well indeed.

A weird phenomena then happened with my own web-shop. The orders were much larger!, and I still don't completely understand why, but it quickly became normal for people to order 3 items or more, with 9/10 of order totals at least GBP£10. Then came the rogue waves, every so often I'd get a customer who would spend silly amounts of money on patches, £100, £200, £300 orders, and I loved those big spenders with all my heart!.

Another strange thing I noticed is that it did not seem to matter to my own customers that they could buy the same product on eBay for half the price. It obviously helps if they just can't find it anywhere else, but I know that's most often not the case at all. What I've learned through my own experience is that, if a customer finds something he or she likes on *your* website, they either simply don't care if it's cheaper elsewhere, or they just don't bother to look anywhere else. Sometimes getting a sale really is just that simple.

The most important lesson here is that there really is a world of opportunity outside the clutches of the big online venues. They like to give the impression that it's all sewn up with no room for anyone else, but they do have a big weakness. They literally are jacks of all trades and master of none. So, if *your* shop is structured in a logical fashion and focused on one theme, or one main area of expertise, it can be much stronger in that area and dominate google search results. I'd encourage you to not be afraid to cut your own niche and own it.

Patch Types

There are currently four main patch types. Embroidered, Woven, Printed & PVC, although recent trends indicate that Vinyl patches are slowly increasing in popularity. This book is focused purely on the production of the Embroidered variety, but I'll also include a brief overview of the other types anyway, just in case you're not familiar with them. There are many reasons that Embroidered Patches are favored over the other types, but it's worth noting that Embroidered is currently the only option where relatively small production runs are possible.

We'll get into the embroidery later, for now I'm going to explain the difference between these four types. It's not my intention to bore the socks off you, so I'll keep it short.

Embroidered Patches

This type of patch was originally made by hand, stitch by stitch, in a very long & tedious process. An average 3" patch design with 50% embroidery contains around 7000 stitches, so both patience and skill were required to make one of these by hand in the old days. Fast forward to 2016 and the same job can be done with a Computerized Embroidery Machine, at the average speed of around 1000 stitches per minute, but there are commercial machines available that can reach speeds of up to 1600 stitches per minute. In this process, the design is stitched on top of the fabric (Polyester Plain or Twill Fabric is the norm), in a 3D type effect. When you run your fingers over the top of an embroidered patch, you can really feel every bump in the design.

Embroidered designs need special preparation before the machine can stitch the design. Each element of the design must be converted into stitches by a digitizing professional, who creates the final embroidery file which is normally, but not always, machine specific. All that sounds more complicated than it actually is, as most embroidery businesses outsource the digitizing process to an embroidery digitizing service. It's worth noting that other types of image digitizing services (for Photography etc.) do exist, so the service used for our purposes is specifically 'embroidery digitizing' only. The cost of digitizing large back patch designs can get very expensive ($100+), but small designs 3" designs can be digitized for as little as $10, so it's entirely practical to make small runs of 10 qty of a small design if desired, with either an Overlocked/Merrowed Border or a Hot Cut finish.

Producing small patches with high detail can be a real problem in Embroidery, especially if it contains small text. When it comes to flexibility of the design shape, Embroidery wins hands down. Just about every design shape you can imagine can be produced in embroidery, and PVC patches are the only other type that offers similar shape flexibility.

Embroidered patches can be finished with a variety of fixing options, Iron on, Sew on, 3m Stick on & Velcro.

Woven Patches

This type of patch is often made with a Jacquard Weaving Machine. There's no base material in this process, as the design is created using a selection of threads which are woven together into a newly formed fabric that incorporates the design.

Woven designs have a totally flat surface (you can't feel the design with your fingers), but it's a bit of a trade-off as when compared to embroidery, as a higher level of detail can be achieved with woven. The set up process for woven patches is quite complicated, and this method is not really suitable for small patch runs of less than 100 qty.

An overlocked border is the only finishing option for woven patches, and complicated shapes or cut-out type designs are not really an option with this production method. They can be made with the same variety of fixing options, Iron on, Sew on, 3m Stick on & Velcro etc.

Printed Patches

This method is seen as the cheap option for good

reason. Originally made by placing simple heat transfers onto Polycotton material to produce a printed effect, they were notorious for fading quickly (sometimes disappearing altogether) after just a few washes. A slightly more robust modern alternative, is to use a Garment Printer with Dye Sublimation Ink, which is a little more durable than transfers. You really can achieve the finest almost Inkjet quality detail with this method, but they won't last forever and the finish is still a little cheap & nasty.

Printed patches suffer from similar issues as Woven. You can't make flexible design shapes and an overlocked border is the only available finish along with the usual selection of fixing options. Small production runs are possible, but as there's not really a lot of money in them, most factories demand large production runs, with a minimum quantity often as high as 500 patches. In reality, most customers will not want more than 100 qty and they expect them to be very cheap.   For those reasons they are usually reserved as a last resort.

PVC Rubber Patches

A relative newcomer to the patch industry, PVC (Polyvinyl Chloride) patches are the solution for rugged all weather patches, as they are totally waterproof and impervious to abuse. The manufacturing process is quite different from the other three types I've described, and this patch type is normally the most expensive of the four types (a 30 to 50% premium over embroidered).

The PVC patch production process requires a metal master plate for every new design, and those plates require CNC milling and are quite expensive to create. Once the master is obtained, the patch is created in reverse, by pouring liquid rubber into the metal mold, in colored layers. The newly filled mold is then placed in an oven/drying machine to finish.

The production process is often done by hand, but very expensive automated PVC badge machines are available to speed up the process. Automation is always nice but you still can't escape the cost of those metal design plates. It is entirely possible to create some unusually flexible shapes with this production method, but it's really only suitable for large production runs of at least 100 qty. For practical reasons, normally only Sew on, Stick on, or a Velcro backing option is offered (as you can't *iron on* a rubber patch!).

I've seen some really cool patch designs made in

PVC, but of all these options, it offers the worst level of detail. I don't want to knock them too much, because I like this patch type for its durable nature, but I do feel that every PVC patch design looks sort of 'cartoonish'.

Overview

That's the four main types of patch, each method has both merits and flaws. I wanted you to read those last few pages so you'll understand that it's the combination of flexibility, durability & the general 3D feel of embroidered patches, that makes them the most practical & popular choice.

 In the past I've teamed up with other factories to offer woven & printed alongside embroidered, but orders for embroidered continued to dominate at a ratio of 20:1, there was no real interest in the other types, so those options were subsequently dropped from my product range.

Backing Options:

There are four main ways to attach a patch to a garment. Iron it on, Stick it on, Sew it on, or use Velcro backing. I'll go through each backing type and explain how & why these options exist.

Iron on patches

Iron on patches are any patch type, Printed, Woven or Embroidered that have been coated with a hot melt adhesive on the reverse side. This is done at the factory during production, in one of two ways. 1) Roll Coated, or 2) Heat Pressed Sheets.

The Roll Coating Process:
A roll coating machine has a hot glue tank which

is fed with small glue pellets, which are melted to form a liquid glue. The machine has hot rollers which are partially submerged in the liquid glue at all times, so the rollers retain a thin layer of hot glue. Once the glue in the roll coating machine is up to the desired temperature (usually around 150*C), the operator takes a freshly embroidered batch of patches and cuts them down into approximately A3 sized smaller sheets. These smaller sheets are then fed into the Roll Coater between the top and bottom rollers and a thin layer of glue is applied. The process normally takes only a few seconds. Once the sheet of patches is out of the machine, the freshly applied glue quickly returns to room temperature and solidifies. This leaves the visual effect of a thin transparent layer of hard glue.

Heat Pressed Glue Sheets

This is my own preferred method for iron on backing, and I normally purchase it directly from a Chinese supplier in 100x0.5 yard rolls. The thickness of the glue sheet is measured in Microns, with the average being 30 Microns thick for Embroidered patch use. I have used thicker & thinner sheets in the past, the difference between them will have an effect on the rigidity of the finished patch.

Glue supplied in this way comes with a paper backing, so there is a glue side and a paper side. The glue side is obvious if it's supplied as a shiny coating, but it's frequently supplied in a dull coating, which makes it tricky to identify the correct side. Fortunately there are nearly always very faint water bubbles on the glue side, so it's possible to use them as an indication of the correct side if you're unsure. To apply the glue, a sheet is cut just large enough to cover the patches. The glue side is then placed onto the back of the patch fabric. The heat press is warmed up to around 190*C, then clamped down for 30 seconds to fix the glue. Once removed from the heat press, the paper is then peeled away to leave the other glue side ready for affixing to a garment etc.

Once this stage is completed, the individual patches are then cut out of the material, either with a laser cutting machine, or simply by hand.

Stick on backing

This is usually nothing more than a 3M type double sided tape (like carpet tape). You need a fairly strong adhesive tape to keep an embroidered patch attached, but it's not hard to find something that will do the job. Even double-sided carpet tape will work just fine.

Sew on backing

This backing option is one of the simplest to create. You can opt to supply the patches with no backing at all, or just apply some iron on stabilizer to the back of them, before you cut them out. There are also other products like Woven Stiffener, which can help to pad out patches that are flimsy/too thin.

Velcro backing

The word 'Velcro' is a very widely known name. Everyone knows what Velcro is, but what you may not know is that it is the trademark of the Velcro Brand. Other companies who offer similar products cannot call their product 'Velcro', some even resort to calling their products 'Magic Tape' or Hook & Loop Tape. I'm telling you this so that you won't miss out on the cheaper alternatives to Velcro, Texacro for example, that also exist.

Velcro tape as we know it, is usually supplied in two forms, the Hook Tape and Loop Tape. The Hook tape is quite rough & coarse, the Loop tape is quite soft & almost fluffy (I've shown examples in the following image). When both parts are stuck together, they form a very strong temporary bond that is useful for many purposes.

For our purposes, it is useful for the temporary fixing of patches to garments etc. It is commonly sewn on, but can also be purchased with a useful 3m type stick on glue backing. The Hook tape is normally fixed to the back of the patch, with the Loop tape fixed to the garment.

What's up next:

If you thought all that info seems good so far, you're in for a treat. You could just simply choose to have fun building a shop and selling retail patches, it can easily become a great little business, especially for those who want a fairly 'hassle free' business that only takes an hour per day to run. But, that's not actually where the big money is, the best is yet to come.

4
BLANK PATCHES

Often overlooked and very cheap to produce, blank patches are both easy to make and highly profitable. I've noticed a significant increase in the demand for blank patches in recent years.

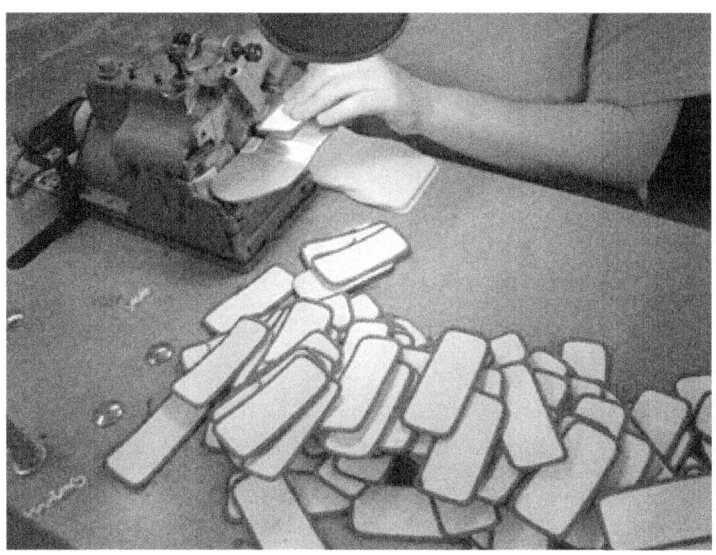

The traditional production method is to cut out the relevant shapes, then use an overlock sewing machine to stitch the borders (as shown in the previous image). The main issue with that particular method is the additional cost of a patch overlock machine at $2000-4000 for a new one. The Merrow company in the USA is a well-known manufacturer of such machines, with the Merrow MG-3U model being the most commonly used machine to add a decorative edge on emblems and patches. They proudly boast that every machine they create can be customized at the factory, so it arrives already set up specifically for your intended purpose. A cheaper option would be to source a used machine. I have occasionally seen very old examples for sale on ebay from around $500, but expect to pay $1500 for a well serviced Merrow MG-3U.

That same company do also make automated badge machines that speed up the whole process. The automated machine versions are a relatively new addition to their range. They incorporate a hopper into which you insert pre-cut fabric blanks. The machine then stitches each edge automatically. It can run through a batch of 100 blanks in just a few minutes, the main drawback is that it's costs from USD$20,000.

If those options seem expensive and not viable, then luckily for us there is a much simpler method available. It's entirely possible to produce blank patches on your existing embroidery machine. All you need to do is create an embroidery file with a zigzag stitch for just the border. Then insert a frame of stabilized material and stitch out the blank borders onto the material. Once completed, remove the frame and cut-out the blanks just as you would any other patch with a hot cut border. Seal the edges with a hot knife and they are ready to sell at $0.50-1.50 per average sized 3 inch blank.

You can easily make hundreds of blanks per day, with just one embroidery machine. Blank patches can be sold individually, or in multi-packs. Production costs are minimal, with the main cost being polyester fabric and embroidery thread. The fabric can be purchased for as little as $1.70 per meter, and it typically come in rolls of 1.5m x 1m. That makes it entirely possible to get several hundred blanks out of just one meter of material. I'll let you do the math's on that example. I do know of some patch-makers who make only blank patches and nothing else, so it is a viable product to sell online and there is a real demand for it.

People who purchase blank patches, generally do so for one of three reasons.
Reason 1: To embroider onto. Either by hand or by machine embroidery.

Reason 2: Vinyl patches. The main design is created via the cut-vinyl process, then it is simply stuck onto a ready-made blank patch.

Reason 3: Dye-Sublimation. The design is printed directly onto the patch via either sublimation transfers, or a garment printer.

For these reasons you'll want to make two types of blank patch. Standard blanks and Printable blanks.

Standard blank patches are made with a plain polyester fabric and are suitable for both Embroidery and Vinyl patch making. In addition to a standard range of border colour's, they can also be sold in a wide variety of background fabric colour's.

So, if you had 10 shapes, in 3 sizes, 10 border colour's and 10 background colour's, it's possible to create a very large range of this type of blank (those numbers would have created a range of 3000!). Easily enough to fill an online shop.

Printable blanks are created in the same way, but utilizing dye sublimation fabric (Pro tip: Duchess Satin fabric works best for printable patches!). The dye sublimation process is best suited to printing on a White background, so that's probably the only fabric colour you'll need for them (although it's also possible to print on other colour's). Then just create the same range of shapes, sizes and border colour's etc, as you would for standard blanks.

Making and selling blank patches in probably the easiest way for any beginner to start making money quickly with an embroidery machine. It requires very little experience and involves relatively simple processes. I'll put some blank patch making tutorials on the Embrocraft Youtube channel to help you along.

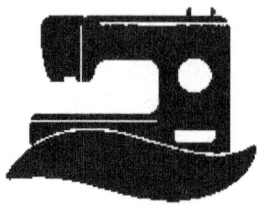

5
CUSTOM PATCHES

Starting a custom patch business was one of the best things I've ever done. But, before you get ahead of me, I must caution you to curb your enthusiasm for just a little while, for this is not a business for the faint of heart. It takes experience, skill and patience to get to the point where you can offer a service of this type with confidence. Many people already skilled in the art of machine embroidery will avoid starting a custom patch business like it's the plague.

Patrons of this business type are notoriously demanding, fussy and sometimes difficult to work with. But I can attest to the fact that those labels really only apply to the experienced users of such services. The truth is that for me, they accounted for only 1 in 10 new customers. The majority of my customers were new to the process themselves and thus, less fussy and more open to workable solutions and alternatives.

The weird thing about working by email is that you quickly gain the ability to read people and their personalities, even from just a short conversation. Within a few months you will almost certainly be able to tell in advance who is going to be a pain in the ass to deal with and possibly avoid taking the order (it goes against the grain to not accept an order, but sometimes it's just not worth the hassle).

For me such decisions should always be taken at the earliest possible stage, preferably before you've wasted time and money on their project.

There are many aspects of this business that don't always make sense. Let's take for instance large orders versus small orders. I've done plenty of both types and while many custom patch businesses will demand a minimum order quantity to ensure an order is profitable for them, I quickly discovered that a minimum order only really matters if you use the same pricing model as the big boys.

The minimum order from most patch companies is 50-100 patches of any new design, but my customers frequently wanted just small runs of 10 patches etc. So it quickly became obvious that an unserved niche existed and it was easily available to any brave fool who dared to take it on.

I do want you to remember that 'if you do what everyone else does, you'll have what everyone else has', and that's usually not very much. Sometimes you need to step outside the box and do your own thing. There is always going to be a risk that your plan won't work, but that same fear is also what's pushing out potential competitors and stopping them from trying.

The industry standard pricing structure usually looks something like this:

One-time design set up fee = $80
Production costs = $1.70 per patch.
So an order of 100 patches would cost $250, then a re-order of 100 qty would cost $170.

The problem with this method is that even with a minimum order of just 50 qty, the cheapest this project will initially cost is $155, with a re-order of 50 qty costing $85.

That 'sort of' works for some project types, but is completely unsuitable for others, particularly from the customers point of view.

The problems become apparent when you realize that most new customers often only want 10 to 20 patches of most designs, but are being forced to purchase 50 or even 100 with many companies. If those same customers ever come back, they will frequently want either a brand new design or at least a variation of the previous design. They will inevitably get stung again on the re-order.

Customers who come back for a re-order of the exact same design are much rarer than you'd expect, so they are paying through the nose every time. Business may be business, but some things can often seem unfair to the customers, and without them, you are stuffed. When most other patch companies were losing most of those people who didn't want 50-100 patches, I tried to find a way to win them over. They started coming to me in droves and they told their friends and came back time and again with new designs.

The Game Changer

The normal pricing methods associated with custom patches does not favor small orders, so in the quest to find a method that did work, I created my own pricing structure based around the industry average cost for 100 patches, which in the UK is around £250 for 100 qty @3 inches. Prices are very similar in the USA (about $250 for 100 qty). I will confess that whilst I have made quite a few orders for customers in the USA (I once made a huge project for a well-known country music festival in the USA), most of my customers have been in the UK and EU. The rest being scattered around the world in various countries.

When it came time to create a new pricing system, all I did was to remove the minimum order but retained a minimum charge of GBP£40 (USD$50) to ensure every project was profitable. If the customer could only supply a rough image, then I would maybe charge an extra £20 (USD$25) to clean up their artwork.

The pricing structure was based on the simple principle of 'discount for quantity' and looked something like what is shown below. Please note that there is no allowance for further discounts other than what is shown. If they want them to work out cheaper per patch, they must simply place a larger order.

1 qty = £39
5 qty = £49

10 qty = £59
25 qty = £99
50 qty = £145
100 qty = £199
250 qty = £395
500 qty = £695
1000 qty = £1250

That particular pricing structure tends to push customers into placing orders of around 25 qty, which is very profitable. An average of £4 ($5) per patch is a very good yield and especially helpful if you are a just starting out and don't have many machines. At that rate each machine can make you £100 to £400 per day ($120 to $480).

If you start a business of this type with just one embroidery machine, you will quickly run into trouble. The amount of money you can make in a day is linked directly to how many patches you can produce in one day, so capacity is everything.

For that reason I'd recommend an absolute minimum of one multi-needle machine + one single needle machine. The multi-needle machine can easily chew through difficult designs that contain multiple color's, the single-needle machine is better suited to one or two colour projects.

If you have one machine of each type you have effectively doubled your capacity, but one of those machines will cost significantly less than the other. A fairly basic multi-needle will set you back around £6k, a single needle can be purchased from just £1k.

The temptation when you're just starting out, is to buy lots of single-needle machines to increase capacity quickly, but that will only get you so far. It is possible to make large production runs of designs with multiple color's on small single-needle machines, but it's time consuming and far from easy. For some people it's a cheap way in and might be worth the hassle, so I'll explain how that's done in the Embroidery Training chapter.

That's really all there is to the standard price guide, but as every order is different, you need to make adjustments up or down depending on several factors. Now, before I explain further, you need to know that embroidery businesses frequently do not disclose exactly how they have calculated their prices, with many going to great lengths to hide that information.

Project quotations are often produced by

calculating many different aspects of the job, including stitch count, materials, backings, machine time and extra finishing work, also how fast the customer needs them can also have a significant effect on the overall cost. Many will use overly complicated algorithms to come up with that price. You can make it as easy or as complicated as you wish, but if you have a base price list to work from, it can all be simplified if you use that as a starting point, then just price things according to project difficulty.

Every project is different and some projects are much easier than others, so a simpler way is to just roughly guess the embroidery coverage. You can easily do that by looking at a design and working out approximately how much of it can be filled with a colored background fabric.

I've shown you four different designs in the next image and they all have one thing in common. They are all stitched mainly with White thread on a Black background fabric. The Black background fabric remains unstitched. So it effectively is made as an applique of sorts.

This is how we make designs profitable to produce, by first utilizing a colored fabric in place of stitches, then just stitch the rest of the design onto it and add a border. Reducing the stitch count can make a huge difference to how long a project will take to complete, and using colored fabrics is just one of the ways we do that.

It may surprise you to learn that we patch-makers do not like to make designs with full embroidery coverage. It is both time consuming and unprofitable, so we avoid it whenever possible. A single embroidery machine can only make so many patches in one day. That could be anything from 30 to 100 qty of 3 inch patches per day, depending on the machine used and the embroidery design. All things being equal, the more patches you can make in a day, the more money you will make, it really is that simple. If you wish to get around this, and increase production capacity, you will need more machines. Embroidery machines are pretty expensive, so it's best to set a pricing structure that factors in project difficulty from the outset.

Having said all that, occasionally you will face a common problem that I've seen many times. A difficult design may take 3x longer to produce than an easy one, but you'll never get away with charging 3x more for the job. Your customers will only be prepared to pay so much before it becomes too expensive and unworkable. It's only prudent to strike a balance between charging a bit extra and still getting the order. In those circumstances you may just have to accept that some projects will take much longer than normal to make and take the inconvenience on the chin.

How to price projects with multiple designs

Embroidery businesses generally charge on a 'per design' basis. If a projects contains more than one design, it's best to calculate each design as a separate project, add all the projects together, then apply an overall discount. I usually knock about 30 percent off the total.

I'm reminded of a recent project I made for Universal Studios. It contained a whopping 32 separate designs and they wanted just 10 qty of each. They supplied vector graphics for all the artwork, so it made life much easier.

There are times in this business when you have so much work coming in that you can afford to be picky about which projects you take on. I already had enough projects to keep my 8 embroidery machines (4 single +4 multi's) busy for 6 weeks, so when I quoted for it, I didn't really care too much if I got the order. You are always strongest when your order book is full, so at times like that you can increase profits without really charging any extra, just by simply not offering a discount. I'll show you how I priced the order.

I normally absorb the cost of embroidery digitizing, but the potential bill was a significant chunk of money at £320 (USD$400). When you add in the knowledge that very few companies would tackle a project of this type, I added the digitizing cost onto the quote to make it a sweeter deal for me.

32 x 10 qty @£49 = £1568 +£320 = £1888

When it came to discounts, I never offered and they never asked. The quote was accepted and I added it to the production queue, then eventually knocked out the project in less than a week. Sometimes it really is that easy. The big surprise is that the total cost of threads & materials to make those 320 patches, was just £24 (USD$30).

Smaller orders equal bigger profits

This particular business is a little different than most others, in that rather than aiming for huge orders that will take weeks to produce, it's far more profitable to make lots of small orders. The advantage that you will have is that larger businesses have the big overheads to match, so they need those big orders to keep the wheels turning. You don't!. That puts you in the right zone to make some good money, and the real bonus is that you're only taking on those small orders that the big boys don't want. There is very little competition on orders of less than 50 qty, and if priced in the right way, they are among the most profitable orders of all. Which leads me on to another area of profitable orders.

Simple Text Patches

These are simple badge designs that only contain embroidered text. Text patches are easily the most profitable embroidered products to make. They frequently contain just a single line of text in just one thread colour. I still keep a few Brother NV800e embroidery machines, specifically for this purpose. Just one of those £1k machines can stitch-out up to 200 simple text patches per day.

To make the embroidery file you will need embroidery software. There are free programs out there, but I prefer to use Brother PE design for this task. It can detect just about any True-Type-Font that you install on your PC and will attempt to create embroidered letters with it. Occasionally you'll try a font that does not work, but for the most part, the majority of TTF fonts can work quite nicely.

Having PE Design installed on a windows PC, will allow you to start creating custom text designs with no previous experience and very little effort. There are tricks you can learn to increase the quality and make things work more efficiently, so I'll put a few video tutorials on this topic on the Embrocraft Youtube channel to help you along.

There are hugely successful sellers on Ebay who only sell custom embroidered text patches. If you can get lots of small orders for custom text badges it's a very profitable business to run. This is exactly how most people start into custom patch work. They get into this area first and learn the logo stuff later. If all you ever did was to buy one single needle embroidery machine for £1k, and a heat press for £250, then made small text patch orders 5 days per week. You could easily make $10k per month with that set up.

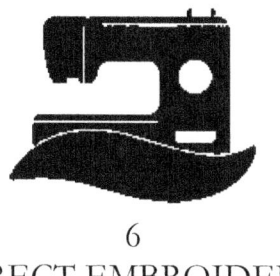

6

DIRECT EMBROIDERY

Direct embroidery is any project where the logo is embroidered directly onto the item, unlike embroidered patches, which are really only an add on accessory . There are several ways you could use this process to create a business.

Contract embroidery is a service offered by a business to embroider goods the customer has supplied. It's a service often used by well-known brands to get their logo stitched onto garments etc. A company offering contract embroidery would normally just sew customer designs onto wearables. The customer usually supplies the items to the factory and then only pays for the embroidery service itself, school uniforms are a popular product of this type. Direct embroidery demands both knowledge and experience. If you make an embroidered patch and subsequently find a flaw, it's easy to just bin it and make another. If you embroider a logo onto an expensive item of clothing and then discover a flaw, you've most likely destroyed the whole item.

There's not much room for mistakes and simple errors are easy to make. Allowances must be made for many new factors. The garment fabric, logo distortion, position and angle, must all be done to perfection.

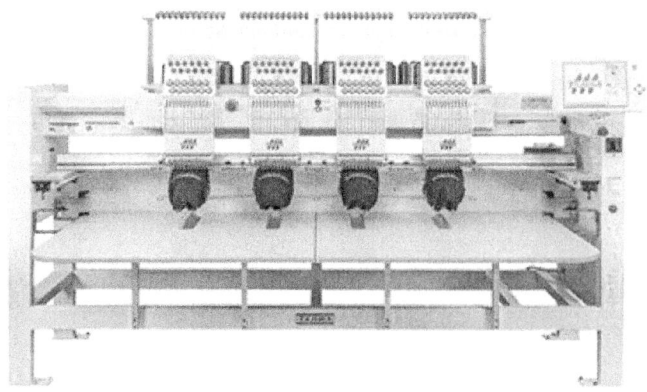

Embroidered Products

If the prospect of dealing with other people's projects fills you with dread, then there's always the option of buying in items to embroider yourself. Baby clothes, training shoes, school bags and teddy bears are just a small selection of the types of product you can create. You are only limited by your own imagination.

Start your own clothing brand

It's much easier than you'd think. All you really need is a catchy business name that isn't trademarked. A cool logo and a range of suitable garments to embroider on. Build an online shop and you're ready to sell. If you promote that shop every which way you can, then you might just hit on something good. Strangely the custom patch business brings in a lot of orders from people who are looking for a cheap way into creating their own branded products.

Here's a quick example of a branding idea:
(Please note that it's a fictitious brand, I just made all of that up as an example).

Brand Name = 'Great Golfer'
Theme = Golf
Customers = Golfer's and golf club pro shops.
Products = Shirts, Tees, Polo's, Jackets, Jumpers, Socks, Trousers, Shorts, Hats, Golf Bags, Club Covers, Umbrellas etc.

I do believe that it works best if you have a theme (like 'golf' for example). That way you already know both who your customers are and where to find them. Who wouldn't want to wear a branded shirt that says 'Great Golfer'. Obviously people associate themselves with brands for many reasons, that's why we have brand snobs, but some of those people would also identify with that 'Great Golfer' tagline. I have probably just hacked into their innermost desire to be a better golfer, and that's when my fictional brand would get the sale.

At the other end of the spectrum, you could target overweight bikers with your...

'Too Fat To Be Gay' range of embroidered hoodies. (I have actually seen that design for sale!)

There are endless possibilities, you only need to come up with an idea that has all the right ingredients, to have the best chance of working. There will never be any guarantee of success, a 'good chance' is often all that anyone can really hope for. The big boys frequently put out new products that don't sell very well, they just become part of your product catalogue, and that catalogue of products will always contain fast & slow selling items.

Production

Everybody's first choice is always direct embroidery, but that can be a very expensive option with little room for discounts. Direct embroidery can cost £6 to £12 per logo, regardless of quantity, which makes embroidered patches a much cheaper option. However, if you have your own multi-needle embroidery machine, your costs would be minimal. A good quality polo shirt can be purchased in bulk for just £3-£4 each. If sold without a logo, you might get £10 per unit, but if embroidered with your own branded logo being sold via the right outlet, you might be able to command a premium sale price of £25 to £35 for the exact same shirt.

Here is one selling related tip to etch permanently into your mind. The selling price of an item is not just determined by the branding and quality of the item. The sales venue/outlet can ultimately have the largest impact on your final selling price.

An example of this would be to take my previous fictional golfing brand and try selling one of those items at various locations.

Here's how it would look:

'Great Golfer' Embroidered Polo Shirt.
Ebay = £15 + free delivery
Amazon = £20 + free delivery
Greatgolfer.com online shop £25 +£5 delivery
Pro Shop at any actual Golf Club £35

You can clearly see that there's a world of difference between those options. I will freely admit that some venues have sheer volume of traffic in their favour, but that can also bring some fierce competition to deal with. Ultimately there is always a right and wrong place to sell anything. Take the antiques trade for another example. I know someone who had an old wooden clock that he found in his grandfather's attic. He took it to his local antiques dealer who offered him £50 for it, which he declined. He then took it to a local antiques auction who told him that he might expect to get £100 for it, which he declined. A few months later he heard about a clock collectors auction in a nearby town and decided to auction his clock with a reserve price of £100. The clock went up for auction and fetched £500.

While that story had nothing to do with selling branded products, it demonstrates the important principle that in order to achieve the best price, you need to put the product directly in front of the most suitable people.

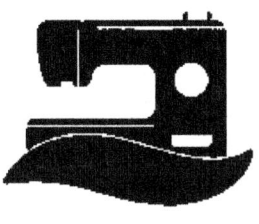

7

PERSONALIZED PRODUCTS

Custom embroidered products are yet another area of embroidery available for those who wish to offer more specialized products. The list of items that can be embroidered is endless.

For personalized products you have the options of both direct embroidery and embroidered patches. Embroidered patches are often an easy solution for products (like teddy bears etc), that are too difficult for direct embroidery. Sometimes it's just easier to create the design as a patch, then stick it onto the item. These types of custom projects are often the most challenging, so it's nice to have both of those options at your disposal. Regardless of which embroidery method you are employing, the rates you charge will most likely be the same. Embroidering directly onto products is quite truthfully not my area of expertise, but many of the principles are the same. The product options for customizing are extensive. Here's a quick list to give you some ideas.

Baby Bibs
Baby Closes
Baby Blankets
Stuffed Animals (think 'build a bear')
School Bags
Lunch Bags
Sports Bags
Towels
Dressing Gowns
Pillow Cases
Duvets
Key Chains
Luggage Tags
Dog Harnesses
Overalls
Fleeces
Jackets
Hoodies
T-Shirts
Polo Shirts
Sweatshirts
Baseball Caps
Beanie Hats

Bucket Hats
Shirts & Blouses
Sportswear
Trainers
Schoolwear
Backpacks
And anything else you can think of.

This type of business is often combined with other personalized product services like Sublimation printing & Hot Foil Printing.

Setting up a business that incorporates many different services might just appeal to those who already have an existing business or possess some experience of making other types of personalized products. It's entirely possible to create an enormous business that combines all of those services into a one-stop custom shop.

8
EMBROIDERY DESIGNS

Modern embroidery work is normally implemented with the help of an embroidery machine. All modern embroidery machines require you to input a design/pattern via a USB flash drive (embroidery cards are no longer used in modern machines). All designs must first be digitized with Embroidery software before your machine can use them. Embroidery digitizing is the conversion of digital images into stitches.

This is a skilled profession in itself and Embroidery software is notoriously very expensive. For many people just starting out those initial costs are quite prohibitive, so thankfully there is an alternative option. Instead of spending all that money and going through months of training, many embroidery machine owners choose to outsource the task of digitizing to a service provider. This quite obviously saves both time and money, but more importantly, it ensures that the quality of the machine output is 'as good as it can be'. Poorly digitized designs are frequently the source of many problems, so it's often best to outsource this part of your project to a professional.

Embroidery file formats broadly fall in to two categories. The first, source formats, are specific to the software used to create the design. For these formats, the digitizer keeps the original file for the purposes of editing. The second type, machine formats, are specific to a particular brand or model of embroidery machine, they contain primarily stitch data (offsets) and machine functions (stitch, trims, jumps, etc.) and are thus not easily scaled or edited without extensive manual work.

However, because these files are easy to decode, they serve as easy exchange formats, with some formats such as Tajima's .dst and Melco's

.exp being so prevalent that they have effectively become industry standards and are often supported directly by machines built by rival companies, or through provided software to convert them for the machine.

Many embroidery designs can be downloaded in popular machine formats from embroidery websites. However, since not all designs are available for every machine's specific format, some machine embroiderers use conversion programs to convert from one machine's format file to another, with various degrees of reliability.

A person who creates a design is known as an embroidery digitizer or puncher. A digitizer uses software to create an object-based embroidery design, which can be easily reshaped and edited. These files retain important information such as object outlines, thread colours, and original artwork used to punch the designs. When the file is converted to a stitch file, it loses much of this information, rendering editing difficult or impossible.

Software vendors often advertise auto-punching or auto-digitizing capabilities. However, if high-quality embroidery is essential, then industry experts highly recommend either purchasing solid designs from reputable digitizers or obtaining training on manual digitizing techniques.

Editing embroidery designs

Once a design has been digitized, an embroiderer can use software to edit it or combine it with other designs. Most embroidery programs allow the user to rotate, scale, move, stretch, distort, split, crop, or duplicate the design in an endless pattern. Most software allows the user to add text quickly and easily. Often the colours of the design can be changed, made monochrome, or re-sorted. More sophisticated packages allow the user to edit, add, or remove individual stitches. Some embroidery machines have rudimentary built-in design editing features.

Loading a design into the machine

After editing the final design, the file is loaded into the embroidery machine. Different machines require different formats that are proprietary to that company. Common design file formats for the home and hobby market include ART, CND, DST, EXP, HUS, JEF, PES, SEW, SHV and VIP. Embroidery patterns can be transferred to the computerized embroidery machines through cables, CDs, floppy disks, USB interfaces, or special cards that resemble flash or compact cards.

Embroidery File Types

File Type/Extension	Company/Machine compatibility
10o	Toyota
ART	Bernina Artista
ASD	Melco
CND	Melco Condensed
CSD	POEM, Singer EU, Viking Huskygram
CXM	Proel TSI, Millennium X
DAT	Barudan FMC
DST	Tajima, Brother, Barudan, Babylock, Melco, Richpeace
DSB	Tajima Barudan
DSZ	Tajima ZSK
E?? (?? = 01-99)	Barudan Tajima

File Type/Extension	Company/Machine compatibility
EDD	Richpeace
EMD	Elna Expressive
EXP	Melco Expanded, Bernina
F?? (?? = 01-99)	Barudan ZSK
FDR	Barudan FDR
FHE	Singer (Futura)
FMC	Barudan FMC
GNC	Great Notions Condensed
HUS	Viking Husqvarna
JEF/JEF+	Janome, New Home
KSM	Pfaff
M3	Juki B
OEF	OESD Condensed
OFM	Melco
PCD, PCS, PCQ	Pfaff
PEC, PEL, PEM, PES	Baby Lock, Bernina Deco, Brother, Simplicity, Melco
PHB, PHC	Baby Lock, Bernina Deco, Brother

File Type/Extension	Company/Machine compatibility
PMU	Proel, ProWin (Proel TSI)
PUM	Proel, ProFlex (Proel TSI)
RPF	Richpeace Welcome
SEW	Elna, Janome, New Home, Kenmore
SHV	Viking Husqvarna
SST	Sunstar
STI	Toyota/Data Stitch
STX	Toyota/Data Stitch
TAP	Happy (HappyJapan)
TBF, TCF	Tajima
U?? (?? = 01-99)	Barudan
VIP	VIP Customizing
VP3	Pfaff, Husqvarna Viking
XXX	Singer, Compucon
Z?? (?? = 00-99)	ZSK

Embroidery machines range from fairly simple single-needle, single-head machines to vastly complicated multi-needle, multi-head machines.

Whichever machine you happen to have, they all share one common trait. If you put crap in, you'll get crap out. That should be your embroidery machine mantra, the one you'll need to memorize if you wish to quickly get to the root-cause of most design issues. Any previous experience you may have with Adobe Photoshop, Illustrator or similar programs will be helpful, but embroidery digitizing is still a very different animal. There are many peculiarities unique to embroidery that you just don't know about yet. It requires knowledge, skill and experience that you most likely don't have at this early stage. I've been playing with Photoshop & Illustrator for many years and have learned to implement some quite fancy digitizing techniques with Brother's PE design & various programs from Wilcom, the industry software leader. But even today, when faced with a custom project, I'd rather send it out to be digitized by an expert, as some things are best left to a professional. I'm quite happy to make small edits, but why waste half a day to digitize a design, that an expert will do in 20 minutes for £10.

With that aspect taken care of by outsourcing it, your time could then be better spent making products to sell. After many years in the Embroidery industry I've collected my own range of some 4000+ Embroidery designs that I have sent out to be digitized by professionals for my old shop, and they all stitch out better than anything I have ever digitized myself. It is nearly always money well spent. I said nearly, because there is always a small chance you'll find a below-par digitizer, so it pays to send them a few test projects to check the quality of their work. You'll also frequently come across designs that just don't work well in Embroidery. Spotting bad designs before you spend money on digitizing is something you will learn over time. Don't worry too much about it for now, as when faced with a difficult design, a good digitizer will often just create a simplified version.

Stock Embroidery Designs

Embroidery design download shops have been around since the very early days of the internet. There are many enormous websites, some with over 100,000 designs available. The biggest problem with shops of that magnitude is finding what you want. You have to wade through an awful lot of junk to find something good. Even then, you'll frequently be expected to pay anything from $5 to $15 per design.

(The following paragraph is a shameless plug!)

My own design collection is available via the Embrocraft shop on Etsy.com. The products are mainly geared towards the production of embroidered patches and I've put some of them into themed packages or collections. If you need some designs to practice with, they are heavily discounted and represent great value for money.

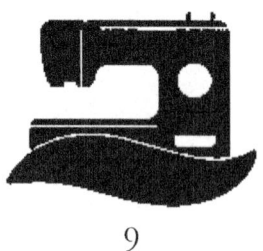

9
EMBROIDERY SOFTWARE

Whilst it's entirely possible to purchase an embroidery design, place it on a flash drive and load it into your machine without editing, you will quickly find yourself needing to make changes beyond what is possible via the very limited options available on the embroidery machine screen. Those basic machine options may be sufficient if you are just a hobbyist, who makes the occasional small project, but if you need to make edits and set up embroidery frames for bigger production runs, you will need embroidery digitizing software. Your computer will play an important role in the setting up of every embroidery design you use, but it's only as good as the software installed on it.

Before we move onto that, I must tell you that in my early twenties I went to college to study as an electronics engineer. Once finished it led to a rather boring existence fixing televisions, video recorders (yes I am that old!) and early satellite receivers (sky etc.). Several more college courses later it eventually led to my own computer repair business, where I gained a lot of experience building & fixing computers. So, I'm not joking when I say that most embroidery software programs are very resource hungry, they need quite a powerful computer to run them on. The computer you currently have may well be sufficient, but will most likely be infuriatingly slow when it comes to editing embroidery designs.   For this reason I'd recommend a computer with the following minimum specs.

CPU: Intel i7 or Ryzen 5 or 7.
You really need at least a modern quad core processor running at around 4ghz to have the power required to edit embroidery designs in a timely fashion. Many embroidery software programs make changes in real time, which leads to the computer freezing up temporarily during even small adjustments.   On a less powerful

computer those freeze ups will drive you mad. Digitizing software is very CPU intensive, so you can never have enough power. I use a Ryzen 7 3700X in my own rig.

RAM: 8gb minimum
The size of the memory is not quite as important as the speed. Faster memory is always better. In my own rig I use 16gb of DDR4 3200.

GRAPHICS CARD: 2gb of any recent model.
Experience tells me that although embroidery digitizing is a graphics related task on the surface, the graphics card does not appear to play much of a role in the resources used for the editing & digitizing process. The CPU will do most of the work. That's good news for you because graphics cards can get pretty expensive. In my own rig lives a fairly basic 4gb AMD Radeon card.

HARD-DISK: Solid State Boot Disk.

If your computer is running an old style spinning hard drive, then you'll need to upgrade to an SSD. It will help your computer and any software installed on it run a whole lot faster. It's easily possible to clone your existing hard drive onto a new SSD, thus retaining all your favorite things. Once completed, it's like fitting a turbocharger to a moped. My rig has a 1tb NVME drive (it's just a newer and faster type of SSD). It makes it lightning quick, with almost every task done instantly. It does not freeze and there is no lag.

Embroidery Software

There are many embroidery digitizing programs on the market, including quite a few free programs. To save you from a lot of heartache I will narrow it down to just two main players. Wilcom Hatch & Brother PE Design. Wilcom software has long been almost exclusively the main choice of professionals in the industry. But it is not easy to learn, it requires extensive and expensive training, it also has a very steep learning curve. You either get to grips with it or you don't, and experience tells me that most people don't. When you consider that the full professional version of Wilcom's digitizing software can cost up to USD$10,000 (that's not a typo), I'd hate to be the guy who bought it and does not understand it. Thankfully Wilcom seems to have realized this and recently introduced a cut-down version called 'Hatch' . You can download a free trial of Hatch on their website, (the full version of hatch costs $1000) and I have used it several times, in the hope that I would learn to love it. But I don't love it, then again I don't consider myself a professional digitizer. For the tasks I find myself doing on a daily basis, it's not really that much use to me. So that brings me neatly to the program I do like.

Brother PE Design:
This is my own personal software choice for editing and even digitizing designs from scratch. It's also fantastic for creating simple text designs, which I have done thousands of times over the last 10 years. It is very easy to learn, everything is just that little bit more intuitive to me. It even has a bunch of free designs & fonts built in.

The icing on the cake for me, is that I run mostly Brother Embroidery machines, so the designs created in the software are already in the correct format for my machines. Outsourced designs are also easy enough to convert into the Brother PES file format. Creating designs, testing and making quick edits is usually a seamless process for me.

I currently use PE Design 10, which now includes a handy function to turn any embroidery design into an embroidered patch. It doesn't get any easier. The latest version is PE Design 11, a free trial version exists and costs from $400.

There exists a market for used software on ebay, so you might find a used example of PE Design, complete with a USB key, for a lot less money. I must confess that I'm a big fan of Brother products, they even make a scan & cut machine that can read the cut lines in an embroidery file. Incidentally, any Brother Scan 'n' Cut machine can be connected to your PE Design software, then you can send cutting files directly to it. They just know how to make life easier for you. I had an issue with one of my smaller embroidery machines last year, it would run for 10 seconds, then cut-out. Over & over again, it was driving me crazy. So I phoned up their customer helpline, fully expecting to get the runaround we've come to know from large corporations, but it never happened. I was put through to an engineer and expected to be told it would be collected & repaired, but that's not what ensued. He talked me through the process to access the engineers menu, checked a few things, then he told me what to clean. I put the covers back on & everything worked like clockwork, job done. I'm finding it very hard to find fault with their products, or their service, even after 10 years.

Regarding software, the only other program I use regularly is a program called Wilcom-Truesizer. It's primary function is to resize embroidery files, which it does very well indeed. I like it so much, I upgraded from the free version and bought the Pro version when it was on a half-price offer for just $50. It can also be used to convert embroidery files between formats. Embroidery files digitized by professionals are generally supplied in several embroidery formats. One of them is usually a .EMB file. That particular EMB file is native to Wilcom software and can be used to resize the embroidery design with very little loss of detail. Once resized, I just save it as a PES file for Brother machines (it can also convert to many other formats). That's why Truesizer is such a handy program to have. The reason I bought the Pro version, is because it has the ability to digitally create different colored background fabrics and insert them under hollow designs. That option makes it easy to create very nice digital previews, which is a useful tool for any embroidery business.

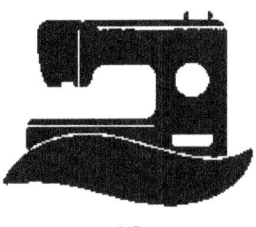

10
EMBROIDERY TRAINING

All this knowledge is of little use to you unless you're prepared to learn how to use it. This can be an expensive game to get into, so I'd recommend purchasing one of the cheaper single-needle embroidery machines from the Brother range first, just for training purposes.

Don't fret too much about spending money that you may not ever get back. Embroidery machines are always in demand, so there is a strong used market with high resale values of all makes and types of machines. The used market may just be where you decide to purchase your first machine. It's entirely possible to buy a used machine, practice on it for a year, then sell it on for the same price. I have bought used machines many times, but I do prefer brand new ones. I'll tell you some of the ways I've bagged a few bargains over the years. Back in 2010 to 2015, there existed a big discrepancy between UK & USA prices of embroidery machines online. Specifically on the Ebay & Amazon websites. Machines that were costing £1000 in the UK, were being sold in the USA for just £300 to £500. The only difference between them being the 120 volt US machine voltage , versus the 240v UK machine voltage. I bought the USA models, imported them into the UK, then simply bought US to UK mains transformers @£20 each.

Over a period of several years I purchased 15 different embroidery machines in this way and I did not just save a lot of money, I also made some money. I generally ran each machine flat out for 6 months, which earned me many times more than my outlay, then I sold them off within the UK for on average 20% more money than I initially paid for them. I made a profit on every single machine. How cool was that. The real trick was in selling them just before they were due the first service, so I didn't have to pay for that. Each machine was sold stating that it needed a service, so there was no comeback.

Things have changed in recent years and while price differences do still exist, it's a bit harder to import them into the UK without getting shafted for import duty and VAT on everything you buy from overseas. But it's good news if you're already in the USA, because those bargains do still exist and you'll be paying a hell of a lot less than people in the UK or EU. Regardless of where you source your machine, once acquired you will be ready to start learning the ropes.

You will find many tutorials on my Embrocraft Youtube channel, but I'd also recommend searching for digitizing tutorials on Youtube, as there are some really helpful videos out there, for whichever embroidery software you decide to use. There is a Youtube channel called 'Colleens Embroidery', and she has a number of fantastic digitizing tutorials, including a complete video series on Brother's PE Design and it's free!. How helpful is that.

Regarding embroidery designs, here follows another shameless plug for the Embrocraft embroidery design shop on Etsy.com. I have created a series of embroidery design packages that are perfect for learning to make patches etc. They are heavily discounted and represent good value. Especially useful if you want to build up a collection of design files to make products to resell etc.

Some embroidery software vendors like Wilcom etc, put on digitizing courses in each country that you can attend and learn the ropes, but they are hideously expensive and I would heartily recommend those previously mentioned tutorials on Youtube as a free alternative.

This chapter is rather short for one very good reason. There is no substitute for experience. You can read this book, then watch hundreds of free tutorials and get a general feel for embroidery, but you will learn nothing unless you buy a machine and practice. Everyone has to start somewhere, and the only way you will learn is by purchasing an embroidery machine and learning from your mistakes. All of the video tutorials that I offer for free via Youtube (there will be quite a lot of them by the end of 2020), they will go some way to helping you avoid rookie mistakes, but it is inevitable that you will make mistakes. Sometimes those mistakes can lead to revelations, it's all part of the learning process.

Now we move swiftly on to the next chapter,

which takes a quick look at embroidery machines.

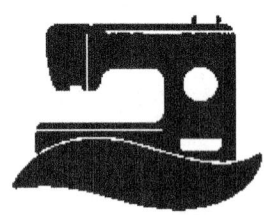

11
EMBROIDERY MACHINES

1828. The year the world's first embroidery machine was invented.

The first known embroidery machine was

invented by Josué Heilmann from Mullhouse, France in 1828. It was aptly named 'The Hand Embroidery Machine'. It was described as a machine that could imitate the appearance of hand stitching.

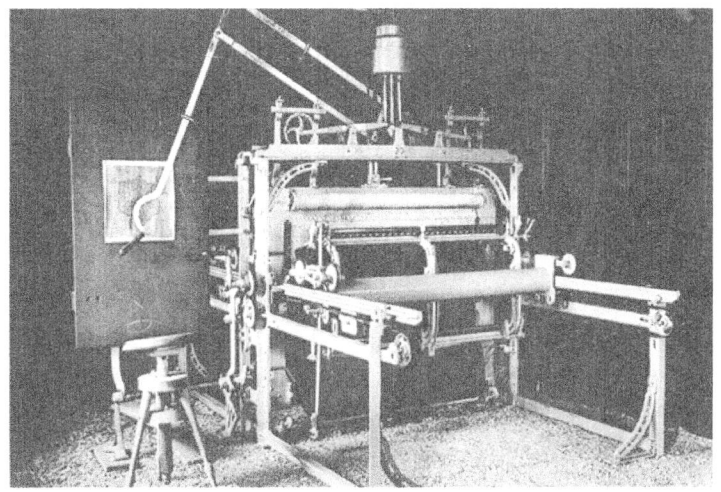

The machine used a pantograph system to transfer the stitches. Each stitch is drawn out on a large-scale design and then its position traced by an operator using a point on one arm of the pantograph. A series of needles responds to the movement of the pantograph arm. Each needle has an eye in the middle for the thread, and two sharp ends. The needle is passed backwards and forwards through the base cloth using a pincer system, imitating the action and appearance of hand embroidery. Each colour in the design is individually stitched until the design is complete. This machine was eventually made in various sizes that were used for both domestic and commercial embroidery. Heilmann's invention was quickly followed by the 'shuttle' embroidery machine and the 'chain stitch' embroidery machine.

The automatic Schiffli embroidery machine was invented in 1898 by Isaac Groebli's eldest son. This dispensed with the pantograph and incorporated a Jacquard system of punched cards to create the design. By 1900, it was fitted with 312 needles, and electrically driven machines were becoming available. These machines were so massive they were only suited for factory use.

Before computers were affordable, most machine embroidery was completed by punching designs on paper tape which was then fed into an embroidery machine. One error could ruin an entire design, forcing the creator to start over.

True machine embroidery dates back to 1964, when Tajima started to manufacture and sell TAJIMA Multi-head Automatic Embroidery machines.

In 1973 Tajima introduced the TMB Series 6-

needle (6 colour) full-automatic colour-change embroidery machine. A few years later, in 1978, Tajima manufacturing had progressed to the TMBE Series Bridge Type Embroidery machines. The TMBE machines introduced electronic 6-needle automatic colour change technology.

In 1980 the first computerized embroidery machines were introduced to the home market. Wilcom introduced the first computer graphics embroidery design system to run on a minicomputer. Melco, an international distribution network formed by Randal Melton and Bill Childs, created the first embroidery sample head for use with large Schiffli looms. These looms spanned several feet across and produced lace patches and large embroidery patterns. The sample head allowed embroiderers to avoid manually sewing the design sample and saved production time. Subsequently, it became the first computerized embroidery machine marketed for home use.

In 1980, Melco also unveiled the Digitrac, a digitizing system for embroidery machines. The digitized design was composed at six times the size of the embroidered final product. The Digitrac consisted of a small computer, similar in size to a Tablet PC mounted on an X and Y axis on a large white board. It sold for USD$30,000. The original single-needle sample head sold for USD$10,000 and included a 1 inch paper-tape reader and 2 fonts. The digitizer marked common points in the design to create elaborate fill and satin stitch combinations.

In 1982, Tajima introduced the world's first electronic chenille embroidery machine, called the TMCE Series. In the same year, they developed the automatic frame changer, a dedicated apparatus for rolled textile embroidery.

Also in 1982, Pulse Microsystems introduced Stitchworks, the first PC based embroidery software, and the first software based on outlines rather than stitches. This was a significant advancement for decorators, as it allowed them to scale and change the properties and parts of their designs on the computer. Designs were output to paper tape, which was read by the embroidery machine. Stitchworks was sold worldwide by Macpherson.

Melco patented the ability to sew circles with a satin stitch, as well as arched lettering generated from a keyboard. An operator digitized the design using similar techniques to punching, transferring the results to a 1 inch paper tape and later to a floppy disk. This design would then be run on the embroidery machine, which stitched out the pattern. Wilcom enhanced this technology in 1982 with the introduction of the first multi-user system, which allowed more than one person to work on the embroidery process, streamlining production times.

In 1983, Tajima created the TMLE Series Multi-Head Electronic Lock Stitch Chenille Embroidery machine, followed by the TMEF Series 9-needle Type Electronic Embroidery Machine in 1984.

In 1986, Tajima introduced the world's first sequin embroidery machine, enabling designers to combine sequin embroidery with plain embroidery.

In 1987, Pulse Microsystems introduced a digital asset management application called DDS, which was essentially a design library for embroidery machines. This made it more efficient for machine operators to access their designs.

In 1988 Tajima designed the TMLE-D5 series embroidery machines, with a pair arrangement of lock-stitch-handle embroidery heads, which were capable of sewing multiple threads.

Brother Industries entered the embroidery industry after several computerized embroidery companies contracted it to provide sewing heads. Pulse Microsystems developed a software product for them called PG1. It was tightly integrated with the embroidery machine using high level protocol, enabling the machine to pull designs from software, rather than having the software push designs to the machine. This approach is still used today. Singer failed to remain competitive during this time. Melco was acquired by Saurer in 1989.

The early 1990s were quiet for machine embroidery, but Tajima introduced a 12 needle machine into their series along with a noise reduction mechanism.

In 1995, Tajima added a multi-color (6-color) type to chenille embroidery machines, and announced the ability to mix embroidery machines with plain chenille embroidery. They also began sales of the TLFD Series Laser-cut Embroidery Machines.

In 1996, Pulse Microsystems introduced the computational geometry based simulation of hand created chenille using a spiral effect.

Following this in 1997, Tajima introduced 15-needle machines, in response to the "multi-color-age".

In the late 1990s, Pulse Microsystems also introduced networking to embroidery machines. It added a box, which allowed them to network and then pull designs from a central server. It also provided machine feedback, and allowed machines to be optically isolated to protect them in an industrial environment.

Since then, computerized machine embroidery has grown in popularity as costs have fallen for computers, software, and embroidery machines.

Many machine manufacturers sell their own lines of embroidery patterns. In addition, many individuals and independent companies also sell embroidery designs, and there are free designs available on the internet.

In the year 2000, Pulse Microsystems introduced Stitchport, which is a server based embroidery engine for embroidery in a browser. This allowed for the factory automation of letter creation.

Although they were not yet ready for it, this transformed the apparel industry by allowing manufacturers, stores, and end users access to customized versions of the mass-produced garments and goods they had previously been buying, with no margin of error.

In 2001, Tajima created heater-wire sewing machines, which were innovative, combination machines.

In an environment that was finally ready for the individuality that mass-customization allowed, the principles developed for Stitchport were adapted in 2008 for the creation of PulseID. It allows for the automation of personalization, even on a large industrial scale.

In 2013, Tajima released the TMAR-KC Series Multi-Head Emrboidery Machine, equipped with a digitally controlled presser foot.

Modern Embroidery Machines

Most modern embroidery machines are computer controlled and specifically engineered for use in embroidery. Industrial and commercial machines and combination sewing-embroidery machines have a hooping or framing system that holds the framed area of fabric taut under the sewing needle and moves it automatically to create a design from a pre-programmed digital pattern.

Depending on its capabilities, the machine will require varying degrees of user input to read and sew embroidery designs. Sewing-embroidery machines generally have only one needle and require the user to change thread colours during the embroidery process. Multi-needle industrial machines are generally threaded prior to running the design and do not require re-threading. These machines require the user to input the correct colour change sequence before beginning to embroider. Some can trim and change colours automatically.

A multi-needle machine may consist of multiple sewing heads, each of which can sew the same design onto a separate garment concurrently. Such a machine might have 20 or more heads, each consisting of 15 or more needles. A head is usually capable of producing many special fabric effects, including satin stitch embroidery, chain stitch embroidery, sequins, appliqué and cutwork.

Moving Forward

Early embroidery machines were primitive and used special tape or punch cards for design storage. Then they moved swiftly through the floppy disk era to embroidery machine memory cards, to the eventual widespread adoption of flash drives as the medium of choice in modern machines.

If you've ever looked at the cost of commercial embroidery machines, they start somewhere in the region of USD$6000 (in 2020) and head upwards toward the stratosphere with top end multi-head machines costing $50,000+.

Then there's the issue of capacity, one machine might get you started, but as embroidery is a very slow process, you're not going to win any races with just one machine. If you plan on tackling larger orders over 1000 quantity in the future, you'll quickly discover that sometimes one machine is just not enough to get the job done within a reasonable timeframe. You can already see why it's a notoriously expensive business to get into, but if you don't have that kind of money, and can't get that level of credit, there are much cheaper options available to you.

New Embroidery Machines

There are a wide variety of embroidery machines on the market in 2020. From cheap domestic machines right up to very expensive multi-head machines. Those larger multi-head machines are really well beyond the scope of this book. It's unlikely that you're going to run out and drop £30k on your first machine. Just about everyone starts out on a single head machine, so we will take a look at domestic and commercial single-head machines.

New Domestic Machines

Domestic embroidery machines are most often the starting point for anyone new to the craft. These machines are usually sold with a 1 year warranty and are classed as maintenance free. That means that you should not normally need to oil or grease them in any way, they just work out of the box. Your local embroidery machine engineer will take of that greasing etc, when he performs an annual service, which will obviously help with the continued smooth running of the machine. All you need to do is clean the machine regularly, removing any thread & lint build up from the rotary hook & needle mechanism.

Domestic machines are a relatively hassle free option, but many of the smaller machines contain plastic parts, where you might expect them to be metal. The most basic machines are slow and tedious, although most will get the job done eventually. A general rule of thumb specifically for Brother embroidery machines, would be that the more you spend, the less plastic parts there will be inside. That's just something I've garnered from my own experience of them. That probably applies to most domestic or semi-commercial machines, as only the full blown commercial machines (like Tajima's etc) will have all-metal parts.

Please note that many manufacturers do also sell what is known as 'combination embroidery sewing machines'. Those types of domestic machines also function as a sewing machine, but the switch over normally involves swapping out parts like sewing feet etc, which for our purposes, would be a royal pain in the arse, so I won't be covering combination machines in this book. The machines we are interested in are 'embroidery only' machines. They are simpler machines, with much less to go wrong.

Having played around with the entire Brother range of embroidery only machines, from the most basic PE500 machines that have a maximum embroidery frame size of just 4 inches and run at only 400 stitches per minute, up to the top of the range PR1050x with 10 needles, a maximum frame size of 8 x 14 inches and run at up to 1000 stitches per minute. A similar story quickly emerges, that's directly linked to the build quality of the machine, ie, how many plastic parts it contains. The less plastic, the longer they will last between services. On the surface that appears to be a simple equation, but the other thing that will affect your servicing schedule is the speed you run them at.

Here's my advice on embroidery speed.
If the Maximum Speed is 400, run it at 350.
If the Maximum Speed is 650, run it at 550.
If the Maximum Speed is 850, run it at 700.
If the Maximum Speed is 1000, run it at 800.

Following that advice on speed will help to prolong the life of your embroidery machine. It will also reduce thread breaks and tangles etc. Do this and it's easily possible to get through an entire design project without any issues.
It will come as no great surprise that the running time between servicing, appears to be seriously affected by the quality of the particular mechanism used inside each model. Luckily the mechanisms used are usually closely related to the maximum speed capability stated for any particular machine (at least within the brother range).

Here's what I discovered.
(TBS = time between services, m= million)
Max Speed = 400: TBS = 5m to 8m stitches.
Max Speed = 650: TBS = 10m to 15m stitches.
Max Speed = 850: TBS = 15m to 20m stitches.

Max Speed = 1000: TBS = 25m to 40m stitches.

Unfortunately my knowledge only extends to the Brother & Janome (which includes Elna) range of Embroidery machines, So let's have a look at some of those machines.

The Brother Range:

Starting with the cheapest and working up through the range, we'll have a look at some of the machines I've just mentioned. Please note that Brother machines do frequently have different model numbers in various markets, for the exact same machine. In your country, the model numbers may be different to what is shown here.

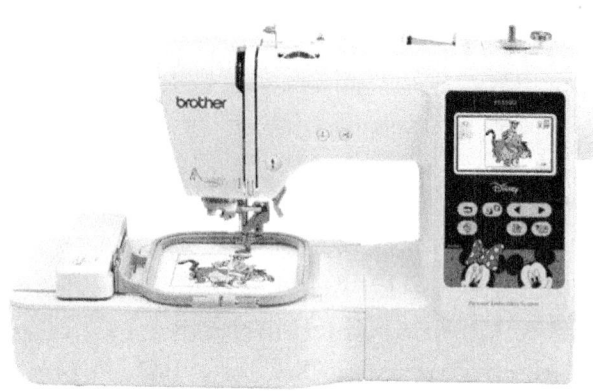

PE550D GBP£799

This very basic machine has been around for many years in various forms. It has been sold under a wide range of model numbers, but from what I can determine, it's essentially the same machine with just minor improvements. They all have the same maximum frame size of 4 inches (10cm), and run at 400 stitches per minute. They are said to be able to run continuously for 18 hours, but in practice, they do not like to be run for more than 6-8 hours straight, before the problems start. Don't get me wrong, they are a very cheap little machine that would be fine to practice on when you're just learning the ropes, just don't expect to do any serious work on it.

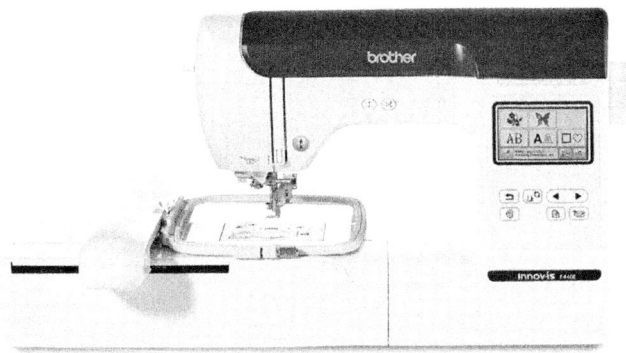

F440E/PE700E/PE800E GBP£999

This machine is the next step up from the PE550D, it has also been around for quite a few years in various forms, in a wide variety of model numbers. It has the same 4 inch embroidery frame, but also comes with a more useful larger 5 x 7 inch frame. Add to that a substantial speed increase to 650 stitches per minute and you have a significantly better machine than the previous PE550D. Having less plastic parts inside, it will run all day without any issues, but 18cm x 13cm is an awkward size for some projects, as you are still limited to just 13cm for circles or squares. Some older models of this machine need to be plugged into a PC to load an embroidery design.

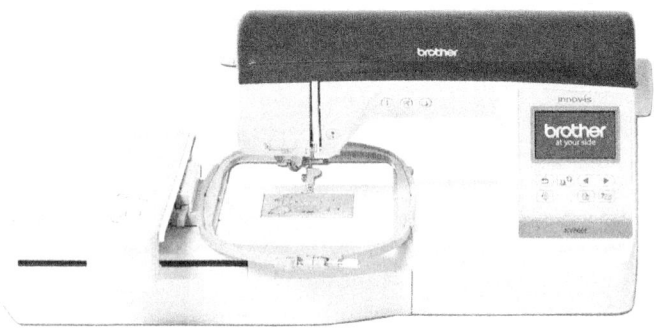

NV800e GBP£1299

Introduced as a brand new model just a few years ago, I've had a few of these machines. It comes with all the same embroidery frames as the two previous models, but with the addition of a 6 inch (15cm) square frame, plus a pretty large 10x6 inch (26x16cm) frame. The embroidery speed is 850 stitches per minute on this machine. It is significantly better built than the two lesser models, the stitch quality is also higher. A handy tip for making these machines more useful, is to remove the blue top cover and fit an external thread stand to your embroidery table, thus enabling the use of larger 5000m thread cones. You can earn some serious money making simple text patches with this type of machine. There are more embroidery machines in the Brother range, but they fall under the category of Semi-Commercial Embroidery Machines. They will be covered in a later section.

Babylock

Please also note that Brother also supplies embroidery machines to the Babylock brand, (Brother do not own Babylock) which is popular in the USA & North America, so you may also find similar machines marketed under the Babylock name.

The Janome Range:

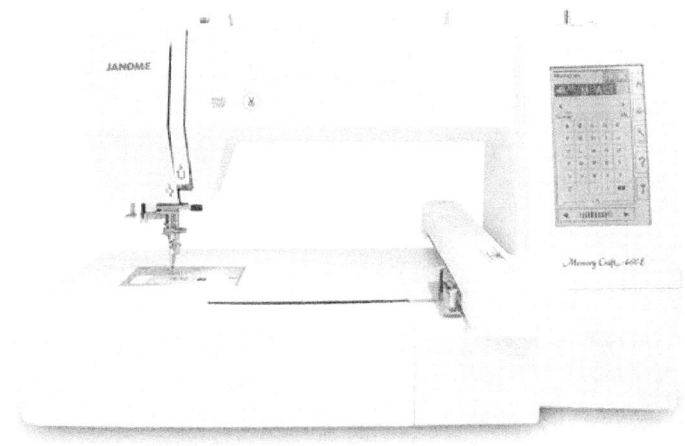

Memory Craft MC400E GBP£999

What I like about this particular machine is that the embroidery arm is on the inside. That makes it much easier to operate the machine sideways on, which can be useful if you wish to place multiple machines side by side. It has comes with a 14cm square frame and a larger 20cm square frame. That makes it more practical than any of the previous Brother models mentioned. Maximum embroidery speed is 860 stitches per minute.

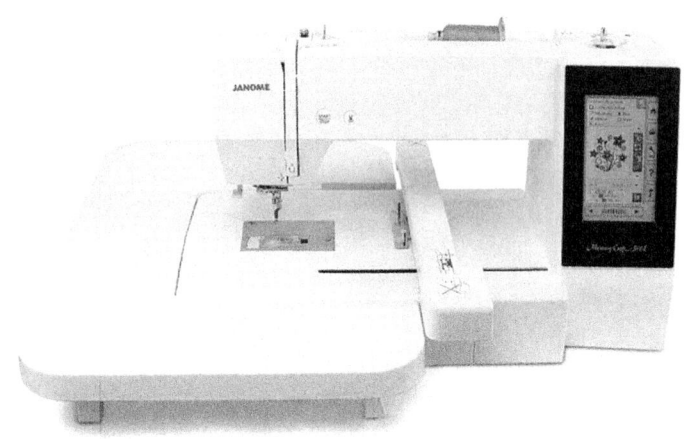

Memory Craft MC500E GBP£1499

Although slightly larger, this machine has similar features to the MC400E, but comes with the addition of a larger 12x8 inch (28x20cm) embroidery frame. Maximum embroidery speed is 860 stitches per minute.

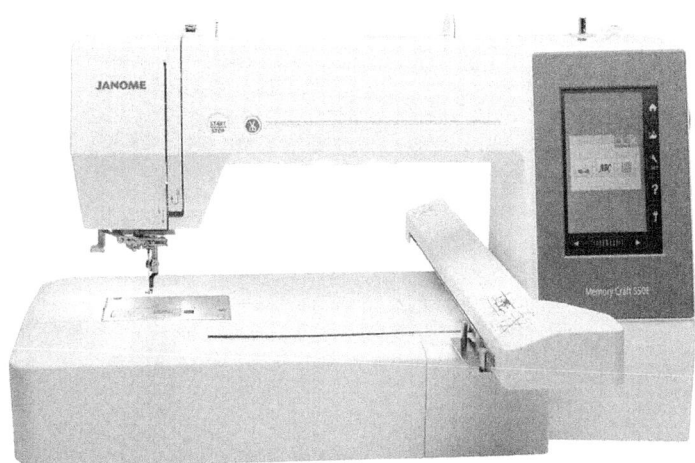

Memory Craft MC550E GBP£1699

Just when I thought domestic machines could not get much better than the MC500E, Janome went and released this monster, the MC550E. It's specs are very similar to the MC500E, but Janome can now lay claim to the largest domestic 'embroidery only' machine on the market. The maximum embroidery frame size on this beast is 14.2x7.9 inches (that's 36x20cm). Maximum embroidery speed is still 860 stitches per minute, but I could live with that. I have no problem stating that this machine is not just good value for money at £1699 in the UK, but also the most practical domestic embroidery machine on the market. I might just be very tempted to buy one of these MC550E's for myself.

The Elna Range:

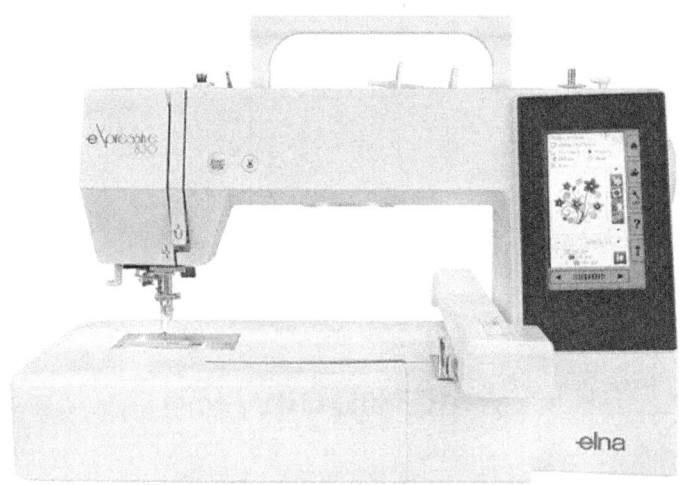

Elna is a Swiss brand which is now owned by the Janome company. Embroidery machines from both brands are very similar are all made at the same factory.

The Singer Range:
World famous for their sewing machines, Singer also make a range of embroidery machines, but I'm not convinced they should have. Everybody loves a vintage Singer sewing machine, but it

would appear that they don't always have the same love for their range of embroidery machines. Specifically their Futura model appears to be troublesome, it does not have a good reputation, so you might want to do your own research into them before taking the plunge.

Other manufacturers:

There are other companies who make domestic embroidery machines like Bernina, Pfaff, and Viking etc. The range of machines is extensive, so it's not really practical to cover them all in this book.

Chinese domestic embroidery machines:

I can easily sum up all cheap Chinese sourced domestic machines with just one word. – Shite.

New Semi-Commercial Machines

Semi-Commercial machines bridge the gap between domestic and full blown commercial embroidery machines. They are hard wearing and will take some serious abuse, so it's worth considering this type of machine. They sit in the middle ground on the road to full commercial machines. They are priced somewhere in the middle, between domestic and full commercial machines, so although a they can be pricey, are generally worth the outlay. All are workhorses with good reputations.

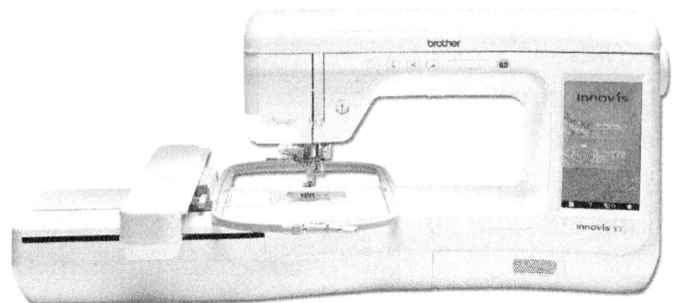

Brother V3 GBP£1999

I have to admit that it still looks very similar to the lesser models in the Brother range, but I assure you that it's a much bigger beast than it looks at first glance. With a maximum embroidery frame of 14x7 inches (30x18cm), there is an optional upgrade kit available to increase that size to 14x8 inches (30x20). There is also a useful 8x8 inch (20x20cm) square frame. Maximum speed is an impressive 1050 stitches per minute.

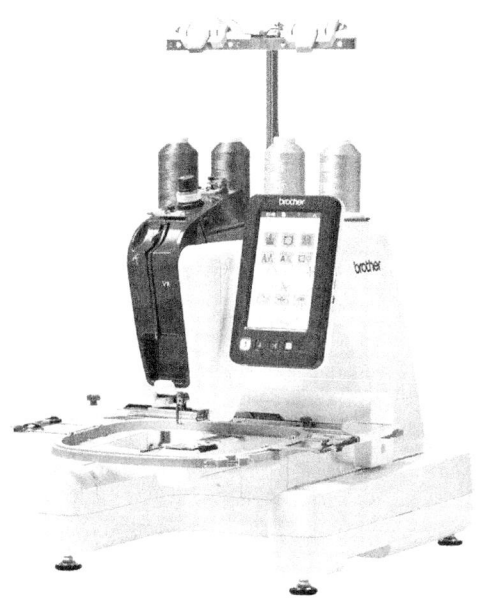

Brother VR Series GBP£3499

Introduced quite recently, this is Brothers 'free motion' embroidery machine. But that fre motion feature is not why you'd want it. This machine is built to the same standard as the more expensive PR range of machines. So you get 1050 stitches per minute with a maximum embroidery frame size of 8x8 inches (20x20cm). From my point of view, that makes it a very reliable machine for simple designs and text patches etc. I've no doubt that it is a very solid workhorse, especially suitable for those who wish to build a text patch business, where you would be making lots of one color designs.

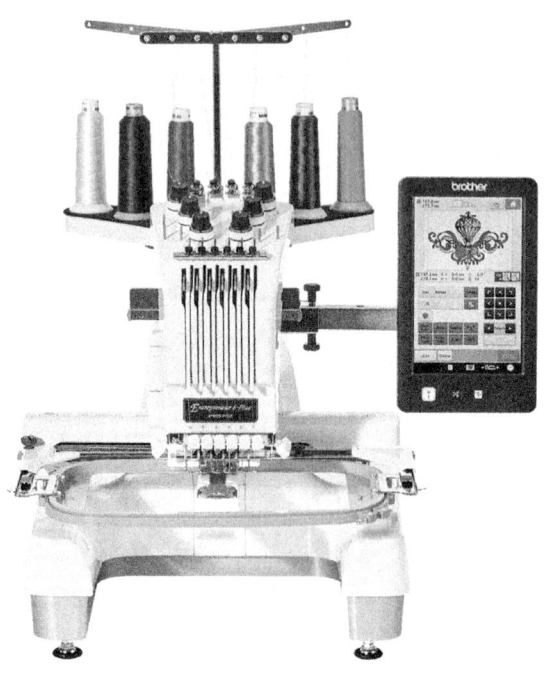

Brother PR 670e GBP£5999
This is the next step up from the VR machine. The same robust construction, but with the addition of 6 needle embroidery. This is the entry level machine most people purchase to get into multi-needle embroidery. It also comes with a larger 12x8 inch (30x20cm) embroidery frame. Extras you can buy include, cap & shoe attachments, plus a cut-work needle kit.

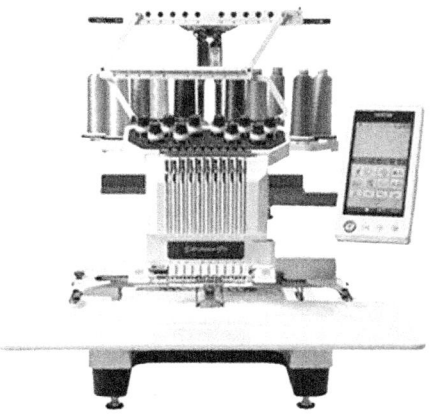

Brother PR1050X GBP£8999

This is the 10 needle version of the PR670e. This newest version now comes with a 14.2x8 inch (36x20cm) embroidery frame. Maximum speed is 1050 stitches per minute. There are always plenty of used Brother PR embroidery machines for sale available everywhere. They have a good reputation for reliability.

Janome Semi-Commercial machines

The MB series of embroidery machines from Janome, has been around for quite some time, so there are always quite a few available on the used market. They are good, reliable machines, limited only by the largest embroidery frame, which is 9.5x7.5 inches (24cm x 20cm) for both models.

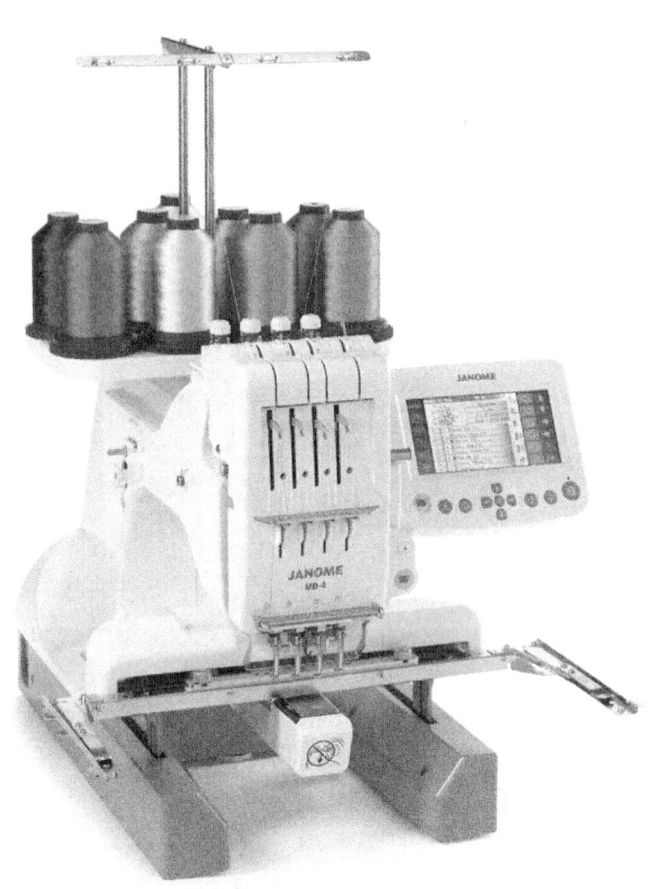

Janome MB4 USD$8499

This is the 4 needle version of Janome's multi-needle embroidery machine. Whilst price checking this model, I managed to find a new one of these on offer at sewingmachinesplus.com for just $4999.

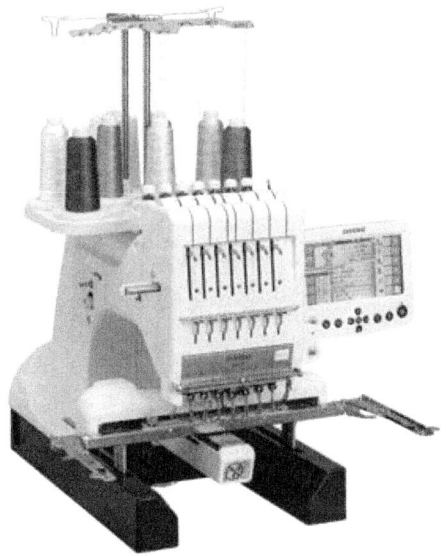

Janome MB7 USD$9999

This is the 7 needle version of Janome's multi-needle embroidery machine.

New Commercial Embroidery Machines

A proper commercial embroidery machine is a very different animal to all of the other machines I've mentioned thus far. This type of machine uses all metal components and is damn near bulletproof. They are designed to run 24 hours a day if needed, and will require maintenance at regular intervals to keep them running. That often involves daily, weekly & monthly maintenance tasks. It may seem a lot of hassle at first, but what it leads to is a very long machine lifecycle, evidenced by the sheer number of 30 year old embroidery machines still floating around on the used market. If you look after them, they will make you money. Big money. Most single head commercial machines will have a maximum embroidery frame size of at least 50x35cm. The average maximum speed of a commercial machine is 1200 stitches per minute. They will run at 1000 stitches per minute all day long, but just like the non commercial machines, it's often better to run them just a bit slower at around 800 spm. That way you'll have very few issues and a longer running time until the next service.

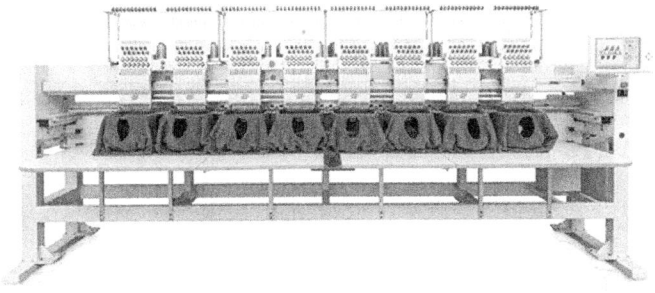

The most popular manufacturers of commercial machines are Barudan, Melco/Amaya, Ricoma, Tajima, Toyota, SWF, and ZSK.

Chinese Cheapies

You will also discover that there exists a whole host of Chinese commercial embroidery machine manufacturers. Often selling for half the cost of the Tajima equivalent they are based on. They appear to be a very tempting proposition. Unfortunately, they are frequently unreliable and you may find it near impossible to get anyone to repair it for you. Most embroidery machine repair businesses are Brand based, so they usually specialize in one specific brand of machine. Once you step outside of that area, you are on your own. For that reason alone you must accept that Chinese machines are often viewed as disposable, so if you take that path, your machine can easily become one very expensive door stop.

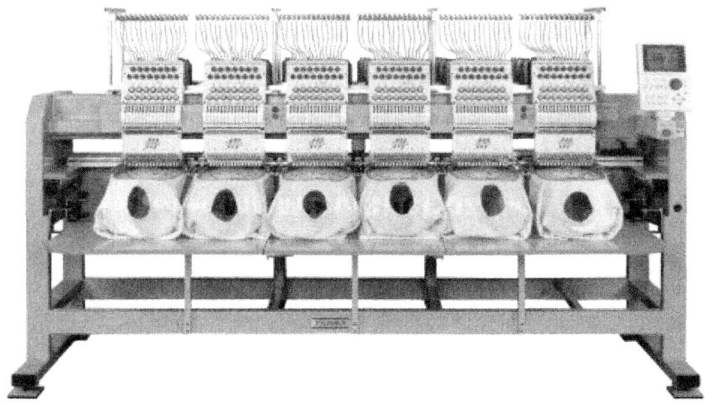

Used Embroidery Machines

Before I close this chapter, I feel the need to offer just a smidgen of advice on buying a used embroidery machine.

Used Domestic Embroidery Machines

Look for a well-cared for example with a low stitch count. People buy embroidery machines, then put them aside and never use them. So you will find loads of second hand machines that have seen little or no use. Good as new domestic machines with under 2 million stitches are commonplace on the used market. So you can afford to avoid anything with over 5 million stitches on it. Not that there might be anything wrong with those machines with more than 5 million, but they are always going to be a riskier proposition. Treat them like a used car, you want low mileage & good condition.

Used Semi-Commercial Machines

Used examples of Brother's PR machines or Janome MB series are always going to be a riskier purchase, but provided you've not paid over the odds, and are prepared to leave it into a dealer for a full service, you should be fine. Spare parts are easily obtained, so there is not a lot that can't be fixed on those machines.

Used Commercial Embroidery Machines

Purchasing a used commercial machine can be a bit of a lottery. You should always demand to see the machine working before parting with any money. If it can't be seen working, then it should be treated as a broken machine for parts or repair and priced accordingly. Don't fall for the old 'it was working fine when we put it into storage' trick. People fall for that on a regular basis. On rare occasions they might even be telling the truth, but you should note that it's also a very convenient way of saying, 'it's not my fault if it turns out to not be broken'.

What to avoid – Chinese Cheapies and anything really old with floppy drives. You want a modern machine that accepts USB flash drives, nothing less will do.

Embroidery Threads

Avoid used embroidery thread at all costs, unless it is still sealed in plastic or free. Embroidery thread starts to deteriorate as soon as it is removed from its packaging. Buying someone's part-used collection of machine embroidery thread, that's been lying in their damp basement for 2 years, is not such a great idea. Buy new thread only, and in 5000m cones (it's much better value). If you have a domestic machine that only accepts 1000m cobs/cones. Just remove the top cover and use 5000m cones on an external thread stand.

Embroidery Machine Bobbins

When your new to this world of embroidery, winding your own bobbins is quite fun for the first few weeks, but you will quickly grow tired of it. That's when you realize the convenience of Pre-wound bobbins. Each embroidery machine will specify it's particular bobbin type. Type A, Type L, Type M etc. Buy the correct type for your machine in Black & White, they are a huge time-saver. Black & White are the most commonly used thread colors. For semi-commercial and commercial machines, that's all you will ever need. Domestic embroidery machine users will most likely still need to wind bobbins for any other colors used.

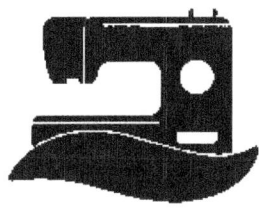

12
SETTING UP A WORKSHOP

Choosing a workspace:

Embroidery businesses are a little different than most other business types, in that we often work very unsociable hours. The embroidery process is a very slow process, so keep in mind that your productivity and potential earnings are always limited by how many embroidery machines you have, and how long they are running for. It is also common for all embroidery businesses to have a queue of waiting orders.

My own experience of running a custom patch business for many years has taught me that your order queue can get out of hand and quickly turn into a backlog of work that can take several months to complete.

If you're just starting out, then your typical working week will often include evenings and weekends. It is also entirely possible that you may choose to take on the occasional rush order, where you might need to work through the night to get it finished. Work of that nature is always optional, but as people are often willing to pay a premium for a faster service, it can also be quite lucrative.

When starting out with any new venture, it's very easy to get carried away on the thrill of that new opportunity, and to quickly end up spending money you don't have. It's much wiser to curb your enthusiasm slightly and approach things in a more logical manner.

What other's do:

I recently had a long conversation with a lady who runs a government-backed business start-up scheme, and she told me about the sort of newbie mistakes she encounters on a regular basis. It usually goes like this.

Local woman has a dream to open a café/diner.

Then she:

1) Comes into some money and decides to live to dream.

2) Finds an empty shop and secures the lease.

3) Spends a fortune kitting it out as a diner. It costs way more than expected due to the extra work required to meet food safety standards and other unforeseen government red tape. She now had no money left, but it's finally ready to open.

4) She opens the doors on the first day and is filled with enthusiasm. All her friends turn up and the place is buzzing.

5) From then on she gets 5 to 10 customers per day during the week and 25 on a Saturday. It's enough to cover most of the bills, but it's early days and she hopes things will improve.

6) Three months later and the bills are piling up, but there is still not enough money coming in to pay them.

7) Manages to secure a bank loan to keep her going until things pick up.

8) Three months later, things haven't picked up and she's run out of money. She's now in the position where she can't pay the bills or the bank loan.

9) Still struggling, she frequently has to borrow money from friends to pay the bills. Bank is losing patience with her.

10) Survives another month until bank loses faith and demands balance of loan in full.

11) Business closes its doors forever.

Every one of you has probably heard a similar story about a similar business in their town. Almost all of them will fall victim to the same problem. Demand. You can start any business and have all the enthusiasm in the world, but if you have no customers, you are stuffed!

In the very early days of my own business, the first online shop I built, also created email enquiries for other things. I had accidentally discovered a way to generate all the customers I would ever need. By making a few small adjustments, it changed everything. I now had the opposite problem to most businesses, I had the demand, but no means of supply. I had been buying all of my products in from other suppliers up until that point, but was now faced with an increasing demand for customized products. That's when I bought my first embroidery machine.

There is an easy way to create a real demand for your services and it's much simpler than you think. I'm getting ahead of myself now, so in a later chapter I will go into finer detail of how to do the exact same thing for many different types of businesses.

It's best not to skip through pages, because in the

interest of delivering value for money for the purchase of this book, I am throwing some REAL BONES at you. It would be a crying shame if you skipped through and didn't catch them. They worked well for me and I've helped a few others to set up similar businesses, so please do pay attention to the snippets I've included. It's nothing but the truth and as pure as the baby Jesus, so read the whole damn book twice if needed.

The gist of what I am trying to say here is; that it's not always wise to rush out and lease premises, or spend lots of money on equipment you don't need. Most people starting out in embroidery, will do so from the comfort of their own home. All you need is a spare room, or even better, a converted garage. For a variety of reasons, I chose to convert my detached garage into two work rooms. An office space and a workshop space, with a stud wall between them. It already had light & wall power sockets, so it was a cheap conversion (Under $1000). Most domestic embroidery machines run pretty quiet, but larger industrials can get a bit noisy. For outbuildings and garages, thick insulation can help as soundproofing for noise reduction.

All of my trade came via my websites, so I didn't

need to worry about customers visiting my home. The only extra visitors were essential collection & delivery services. Back then my kids were still young and I was worried about them going near the machines, so I opted for the garage so I could keep the machinery safely out of harm's way.

Workshop Contents

Your workshop can easily be organized into just one room. All you really need is the bare essentials.

1) A computer & printer (on a desk or table).

2) Tables or stands for embroidery machines.

3) A large worktable for cutting fabric.

4) A small bookcase for thread storage.

5) Somewhere to store fabric and stabilizer.

6) A large heat press (can go under a table).

7) Storage drawers for tools and bobbins.

8) Scissors and fabric cutters.

9) A small table with a A2 size cutting mat.

10) Wall hooks for embroidery frame storage.

11) A good range of fabric.

12) A good selection of threads.

13) Pre-wound bobbins in black & white.

14) Embroidery stabilizer in black & white.

15) A bobbin tension gauge (for semi-commercial & commercial machines).

There are many other fancy tools and accessories you could buy to make you feel better, but you will probably never use them. The items listed above are all that you really need for 99 percent of embroidery projects.

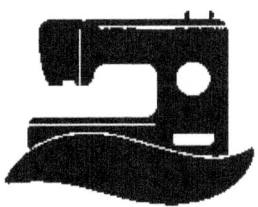

13
BUILDING AN ONLINE SHOP

If you've got this far through the book, but it all sounds too complicated and hard work. Don't worry, I still have something for you. Mainly because the same ideas put forth, can equally be applied to either scenario, regardless of whether you made the products yourself.

You could easily build a simple website to promote your embroidery business, but six pages of content on the web, will probably not attract very much business. Without a regular flow of web traffic you are wasting your time. Every page, product or post, is a window to your website. Those windows can have tags and images that also help to bring traffic. You would be amazed at just how much traffic your properly tagged product images can produce via Google images.

So, the answer my friend, is to build an online shop, preferably with a few hundred listings to create some buzz.

When I built my first online shop, I did so because I was sick and tired of Ebay and Amazon's fees & rules. Especially seller ratings, feedback and all the aggravation that came with it. When you build your own site, the rules are different. You can list as many products as you wish, and they don't cost you any extra money. You also don't pay fees when you sell something, only the payment gateways get a small slice for handling the payment. Paypal takes about 3.9% +0.20p, Stripe offers much better rates at 1.9% +0.20p.

Many people use services like Shopify and Bigcommerce to host their online shop. They do most of the work and you just add listings. I chose the self-hosted Wordpress route, with the shop element being powered by Woo-commerce.

All running on a Virtual Private Server, provided by a well know ISP. It cost around GBP£50 per month, but being a VPS I could add other websites to the server at no extra cost, so it later proved itself useful for other projects.

Whatever your chosen hosting option, your online shop can be used for many different purposes. Here's a few examples.

Scenario 1: Let's say that you're not really interested in making products with an embroidery machine, you're just wanting to start an online business that's sells high profit products and is very simple to run.

Solution 1: Buy in a range of Embroidered patches from China and sell them in your online shop. They can be purchased on Alibaba.com from as little as USD$0.30c and sell for $3 to $5 each. Who doesn't like profit margins in excess of 1000 percent. $1000 in stock will produce over $10,000 in revenue and you didn't have to make anything.

Scenario 2: You want to start a custom embroidery business, but don't know how to attract customers.

Solution 2: it's the same as for scenario 1, you

just add a 'get a quote' page, and maybe an extra page of spiel about the range of custom services you offer. You can then choose between buying in stock or making the products yourself to sell.

The real magic is in the traffic attracted by 500+ shop listings for products that are relevant to the industry you're in. You then tap that traffic by offering a custom service on the same website. This simple system can be applied to any industry where you wish to offer a customized product or a service, just reel them in with stock products, then stick the custom service under their nose. Through helping other people build their businesses over the years, I have tried this method in a few unrelated industries, and I can tell you that not only does it work well, it is a seriously powerful way to build a business.

The Bonus.
You don't necessarily have to provide the custom service yourself. On one of my previous websites, I took care of the retail orders, but farmed out the custom orders to an overseas factory. They handled everything, the quotes, the orders & the delivery. I just got paid a 30% commission on every order sent via the form on my website. You can choose to make it as easy, or as difficult as you like. It's your party.

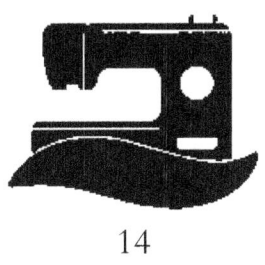

14
BOOK SUMMARY

If I missed anything in this book, it will most
likely be in the realm of embroidery production.
The main reason for this omission is that it's
more of a practical & visual process, and
therefore easier to show you in a series of videos,
than to try to explain it in words. Many of you
will have learned of this book via adverts I placed
within those videos. All I can say to that is
'thank you' for proving that my marketing efforts

were not in vain. For those of you who found this book by other means, I recommend seeking out the Embrocraft channel on Youtube, where you can indulge yourself in hundreds of free videos that I made to complement this book. They are being released as quickly as I can edit and upload them. So please also consider subscribing to the Embrocraft Youtube channel, it will always be a free resource for you. Making hundreds of videos might seem like overkill, but it does generate a lot of traffic and provides a great opportunity to promote a book. People waste bucket loads of money on google adverts every month, when all you really need to do, is create your own videos, insert your own ad, then stick them on Youtube. - Voila!

That's yet another snippet for you. Even if you've got this far and you're still not interested in making money with an embroidery machine, you will hopefully have picked up a few things along the way that could be put to good use in other ways.

If you enjoyed this book, then please consider leaving a nice review on the Amazon website. Now that I'm heading rapidly towards old age, I would rather make my own projects than other people's. But that's purely because I've made far too many projects (over 10,000) for other people. I now want to do more stuff for my own enjoyment and the Embrocraft project is something I have grown to enjoy. That's where the future is for me and when it's all finished I will be glad of the rest.

Thanks again for purchasing this book and for taking the time to read it.

Trev Hunt.

Useful links:
Embrocraft on Etsy:
https://www.etsy.com/uk/shop/Embrocraft

Embrocraft on Youtube:
https://www.youtube.com/channel/UC7GhMfk dH5WJuGZFCM9FYLQ

Please note the YT channel is a work in progress and may not be completed until summer/autumn 2020.

MORE BOOKS BY TREV HUNT

Embroidery Machine Profits.
Embroidery Design Profits.
The Embrocraft A-Z of Fabric.
The Embrocraft A-Z of Embroidery.
The Embrocraft A-Z of Sewing.

ABOUT THE AUTHOR

Trev Hunt has been working in the Embroidery industry for many years. Now close to retirement, he is sharing his experiences with you, in the hope that you too may wish to earn a living in this weird and wonderful industry. He has written five books on the sewing and embroidery industry.

Printed in Dunstable, United Kingdom

70154521R00087